GARVAGHY

A Community Under Siege

To Mom,

Thanks for giving me

to work with folks like these!

Love,

Sky

GARVAGHY

A Community Under Siege

Garvaghy Residents

First published in 1999
by
Beyond the Pale
BTP Publications Ltd
Unit 2.1.2 Conway Mill
5-7 Conway Street
Belfast BT13 2DE
Tel: +44 (0)2890 438630
Fax: +44 (0)2890 439707
E-mail: office@btpale.ie
Internet site: http://www.btpale.ie

British Library Cataloguing-in-Publication Data.
A catalogue record for this book is available from the British Library.

ISBN 1-900960-06-0

Front cover photo: Derek Speirs/Report. 'Orange feet on the Garvaghy Road' 1997. In the background, Garvaghy residents are imprisoned by a wall of British army and RUC vehicles and riot squads, while the Garvaghy Road is cleared for the Orangemen to return from Drumcree Church.

Back cover photo: Mal McCann.

Printed by
Colour Books Ltd, Dublin.

Dedicated to
Rosemary Nelson
fearless defender of human rights

murdered 15th March 1999

Contents

Acknowledgements

This book is the product of a communal effort and thanks are owed to many people. We will not, however, mention them all by name as to do so might jeopardise their jobs, their careers, or their physical safety. With this in mind we would like to express our appreciation to all of those people who gave freely of their time to writing, researching, reading, typing and gathering photographs.

Particular thanks are due to Ruth who urged us on when we had lost momentum and to the GRRC for allowing us access to their files. We are most indebted to all of you whose testimonies we were not able to include, and to the generations before us who never got to tell their stories.

Garvaghy Residents, June 1999.

Rosemary Nelson

This book is dedicated to Rosemary Nelson, murdered on the 15th of March, 1999.

The contributions recorded in this book relate to events arising from the Garvaghy Road campaign over the past few years but are focused on July, 1998. They were written in the month that followed. Since then, the community suffered a devastating blow in the tragic death of Rosemary Nelson.

As a community, we all owe a major debt to Rosemary for her courage in attempting to defend through the legal system the rights of nationalists in Portadown. It was Rosemary's outstanding legal ability, courage and dedication that enabled her to mount a legal challenge which forced the Chief Constable of the day to re-route the Orange parade of July 1996, a decision he later reversed. In July 1996, she used her considerable experience of the law and worked within the law to try and ensure that our rights were translated into reality.

Rosemary was there from the beginning, ever passionate in her concern for the rights of the community; but more so in defending those individuals who were victims of RUC brutality. She never lost her capacity to be outraged when people's rights were abused. She was always indignant about injustice.

For people living on the Garvaghy Road, she was more than just our solicitor. Rosemary was also a friend who not only stood by us, but with us. On those occasions when pickets and public protests were underway, Rosemary was not in her office, but present with the people.

Likewise, her commitment to the family of Robert Hamill is well known; as is her involvement with the families of others killed by the forces of the state or by loyalists with their collusion. Less well known is her work for the Travelling community; on women's rights; in opposing discrimination in the workplace; and on behalf of the Irish language. She also worked with many voluntary and community groups and with local schools in Lurgan. She was also an 'ordinary' lawyer who worked with all sides of the community in Lurgan and beyond on everyday legal issues with dedication and commitment.

Despite her high profile and reputation as a lawyer, Rosemary remained a charming woman whose clients came to feel they were not dealing with a solicitor so much as with a friend. Consequently her killing was felt by many as a personal loss. The Rosemary Nelson that people knew was a very special and rare person.

Rosemary has now adopted a public persona and public controversy rages around her murder. She would be embarrassed and bemused by all the publicity. For there was also a private side to Rosemary. To her friends, she was just Rosie, a warm, thoughtful woman who loved to laugh and enjoyed the craic. A warm, generous and wonderful woman whose friendship is irreplaceable. We are all the poorer for her passing. Most of all, of course, she will be missed by her husband Paul and her children, Gavin, Christopher and Sarah. Their lives have been torn apart and they are uppermost in our minds and in our prayers.

In the aftermath of her murder, it is important to remember those three ideals which Rosemary pursued – truth, justice, equality – and for which she gave her life. It is up to us to ensure a totally independent and RUC-free investigation and inquiry into Rosemary's murder. We must ensure that the truth is told and heard. To remain silent, to ignore the wrongs in our society would be to ignore Rosemary herself. It is up to all of us to campaign for truth and for justice for Rosemary and her family. Rosemary would have done no less for any of us.

Ní bheidh a leithéid ann arís.
Ar dheis Dé go raibh a h-anam.

Introduction

The nationalist community in Portadown has over recent years achieved international prominence from its opposition to intrusive Orange Order marches on the Garvaghy Road. According to Orange Order mythology what is at stake is 'the right to walk the Queen's highway', a walk which 'takes seven minutes'. It is also claimed that only in the past few years has there been any dispute over the parades, a controversy deliberately whipped up by a small group of residents with a political axe to grind.

This book shows that the Orange Order remains one of the central pillars of institutionalised sectarianism in the North of Ireland. It is not the 'right to march' that is being asserted, or a simple 'celebration of culture', as the Order maintains. Marching through Catholic areas against the wishes of local residents is about flaunting the symbols of Protestant supremacy and the culture of unionist domination. It matters desperately to the Orange Order to hold on to some sense of a past in which unionists controlled the economy, government, the civil service, the police and the media, and in which British governments could be relied on to give unqualified support for the Union.

It is no accident that this life and death struggle has been taking place in Portadown. As it is often said on 'the (Garvaghy) road', 'it started here: it will end here'. The Orange Order was founded near Portadown over two hundred years ago and ever since, Portadown District has proven to be the most hardline of the Orange lodges in asserting their 'right to dominate'. Since 1795, Drumcree church has been the rallying point for a pre-Twelfth of July parade through the Catholic quarter of Portadown

– now the Garvaghy area. Periodically, residents have resisted the Orange invasions. The second part of this book describes in some detail the violence associated with Orange marches over the last two centuries, an account which ends with the murder of human rights lawyer, Rosemary Nelson. The historical evidence clearly shows that 'traditional rights' were forged from the wrecking of Catholic homes and property, murder and violent assaults.

The main purpose of the book, however, is to provide *contemporary* accounts in words and pictures of what it is like to live in the Garvaghy area during the 'marching season'. In July 1998, independent councillor Joe Duffy encouraged Garvaghy residents to keep diaries as the time of the Drumcree parade approached. The residents' accounts reveal the accumulated emotions of four years of struggle to get the parade re-routed away from the Garvaghy Road. Year after year, their peaceful protests have been brutally repressed, culminating in the scandalous 'clearing of the road' in 1997 by units of the RUC backed up by the British Army. The authorities made sure that 'Orange feet' were on the Garvaghy Road in July 1995, 1996 and 1997, after widespread Orange protests which, in the words of the North Report, reduced the North of Ireland to 'virtual anarchy'.

With these experiences in mind, the community did not look forward with any enthusiasm to July 1998. However, the decision by the newly-established Parades Commission that the Orange march to Drumcree should return home by its outward route (and *not* via the Garvaghy Road) indicated something of a sea change in official policy. While the decision was welcomed by residents with a certain relief, there was a general wariness as to whether the decision would be allowed to stand and would be upheld. Notwithstanding the reaction of the Orange Order in July, the re-routing decision not only stood for the immediate crisis but remains standing as this book goes to press (June 1999) more than three hundred days later.

As the Americans say, 'there is no such thing as a free lunch!' The price of stopping the march has not been cheap. From the

4th and 5th July, the nationalist community found itself inside 'a ring of steel' and, not without irony, being defended by the very security forces they had grown to hate and despise! The removal of the military defences a fortnight later left them surrounded by a ring of sectarian hatred, with Orange mobs gathering nightly, intent on mayhem.

The stories that follow relate the fears and feelings of ordinary decent people caught up in an extraordinary situation. Between them, they give a coherent account of what it was like during a traumatic fortnight. Reviled as 'Adams' dogs' and 'Mac Cionnaith's animals', and other similar terms of abuse, they reveal themselves as concerned and anxious about the tragic death of the Quinn children and wondering if they had some responsibility in the matter. This is in stark contrast to the callousness of the Orange Order, which refuses to accept responsibility for anything that happened.

What these ordinary people aspire to is being treated as equals, not as a carpet for the Orange Order to walk over. By refusing face-to-face meetings with the Garvaghy residents, the Orangemen are refusing also to see the residents as equals. By insisting on marches where they do not have the consent of the local community, they are denying the right of residents to live free from sectarian harassment. By threatening 'to take the law into our own hands if we have to' and by failing to take any responsibility for the violence and hatred associated with Orange marches, the Order has colluded in killing. The Orange Order was founded on the principle of religious exclusivity and supremacy. It remains a bastion of sectarianism, an archaic citadel which stands firmly against equality and human rights.

Who's Who?

Adams, Gerry: President of Sinn Féin, Member of Parliament for West Belfast, Assembly Member.

Berry, Paul: Democratic Unionist Party (DUP), lives in Tandragee, Co. Armagh, youngest member of the Northern Ireland Assembly member, Drumcree activist.

Bingham, Reverend William: Presbyterian minister in Pomeroy, Co. Tyrone, chaplain to the Armagh Grand Lodge of the Orange Order.

Brady, Archbishop Seán: Catholic Primate of Ireland.

Campbell, Sheena: Sinn Féin local government councillor, murdered by loyalists.

Duffy, Joe: independent nationalist councillor and joint spokesperson for Garvaghy Road Residents' Coalition.

Gilmore, Pauline: spokesperson for ORDER (Ormeau Residents Demand Equal Rights) and loyalist supporter of Orange protests at Drumcree.

Gracey, Harold: District Master of the Portadown District of the Orange Order.

Graham, Alastair: Chairperson of the Parades' Commission.

Hamill, Robert: a Catholic resident of Portadown, father of three, kicked to death by a loyalist mob in Portadown town centre in April 1997, while four RUC officers sat in a nearby landrover.

Jones, David: press secretary for the Orange Order in Portadown.

Mac Cionnaith, Breandán: Former republican prisoner, independent councillor, joint spokesperson for Garvaghy Road Residents' Coalition.

McCrea, William: DUP MP, Assembly Member, associate of Billy Wright (see below).

McGoldrick, Michael: charity worker and father of Michael McGoldrick (jnr), who was murdered by loyalists in 1995.

McGuinness, Martin: Member of Parliament for Mid-Ulster, Assembly Member.

McNarry, David: member of the Grand Lodge of the Orange Order.

McWilliams, Monica: founding member of the Northern Ireland Women's Coalition, Assembly Member for South Belfast.

Mallon, Seamus: Deputy First Minister designate, Member of Parliament for Newry/Armagh, Deputy Leader of the Social Democratic and Labour Party (SDLP).

Mowlam, Marjory 'Mo': British Labour Party MP, Secretary of State for Northern Ireland.

Murray, Darren: 12 year old, killed by a van, October 1996, while running away from loyalists who taunted him as 'the Fenian nigger'.

Neeson, Sean: Leader of the Alliance Party, Assembly member for East Antrim.

Nelson, Rosemary: solicitor to the Hamill family and the Garvaghy Road
Residents' Coalition, murdered by a car bomb, March, 1999.
O'Hagan, J B: veteran republican activist, father of Dara O'Hagan.
O'Hagan, Dr Dara: the Sinn Féin Assembly Member for Upper Bann
which includes the Garvaghy Road area.
Paisley, Rev Ian: MP, MEP, leader of the Democratic Unionist Party,
Assembly member for North Antrim.
Patton, Joel: leader of the hardline 'Spirit of Drumcree' group, expelled
from the Orange Order for militant opposition to the leadership.
Left the Orange Order in 1999.
Quinn children (Jason, Mark and Richard): members of a Catholic
family living on a mainly Protestant housing estate in Ballymoney,
Co. Antrim, burnt to death when loyalists petrol bombed their
home on July 12th 1998.
Rice, Gerard: former republican prisoner, spokesperson for the Lower
Ormeau Concerned Citizens group.
Rodgers, Bríd: leading member of the SDLP, Assembly Member for
Upper Bann which includes the Garvaghy Road area.
Sands, Bobby: IRA prisoner, Member of Parliament for Fermanagh/
South Tyrone; died on hunger strike, 5th May 1981.
Watson, Denis: Grand Master of the Co. Armagh Lodge of the Orange
Order.
Wright, Billy: widely known as 'King Rat', a leading member of the
Ulster Volunteer Force but split from them and set up the Loyalist
Volunteer Force; killed in prison by members of INLA on
December 27th 1997.

What's what?

Belfast Agreement: signed by most political parties in the North on Good
Friday, 1998. Led to elections for Northern Ireland Assembly.
Body alarm: a portable personal alarm set off by the owner if in danger.
Buckfast: strong, cheap wine.
Calpol: a drug in medicine form given to young children and babies;
lowers temperature and aids sleep.
Craic: an Irish word, loosely translated as lively atmosphere, convivial
social ambience.
Croppies: term originating in the 18th century, when Irish rebels wore
their hair cropped short to designate sympathy with the republican
ideals of the French revolution.
DFJ: Drumcree Faith and Justice Group.
DMS: Divisional Mobile Support Unit, the 'anti-terrorist' militarised
unit of the paramilitary Royal Ulster Constabulary.
Dole: colloquial term for social welfare or unemployment benefit.
Drumcree Church: the Church of Ireland church which is the focal point
of the Orange protest.

Fenian: after the Fenian Brotherhood founded in the 1860s to fight for Irish independence. 'Fenian bastard' remains a widespread term of abuse directed at Catholics of all shades of opinion and none.

Fleadh: a traditional music festival.

Free State: following the War of Independence in 1922, Ireland was partitioned. The southern 26 counties were known as the Free State. In 1948, a new Constitution was brought into force for the island of Ireland, declaring a republic. However, the new Constitution contained a proviso (Article 3) that, so long as the six northern counties remained under British jurisdiction, the laws of the republic applied only to the territory of the former Free State. The term 'Free State' continues to be used by many northern nationalists when referring to the south of Ireland. In the referendum of 1998, the majority of voters in the 26 Counties supported the dropping of Articles 2 and 3 from the Irish Constitution. This change was part of the Belfast Agreement.

GAA: Gaelic Athletic Association.

GRRG: Garvaghy Road Residents' Group (later, GRRC).

GRRC: Garvaghy Road Residents' Coalition.

LOL: Loyal Orange Lodge.

LVF: Loyalist Volunteer Force.

Northern Ireland Assembly: set up as a result of the Belfast or Good Friday Agreement.

Parades' Commission: established in 1997 to make decisions about contentious marches; its decisions are legally binding.

Proximity talks: conflict resolution technique in which the parties are in the same place but do not meet, negotiating through intermediaries instead.

Roche 5: a prescription tranquiliser.

RTE: Radio Telefis Éireann, the Irish national broadcasting organisation.

RUC: Royal Ulster Constabulary, paramilitary police force of Northern Ireland which has a 93% Protestant membership.

Saracen: a large armoured personnel carrier used by the British army.

Scarva, mock fight: an annual event, when men in period costume re-enact the Battle of the Boyne, when the forces of King William III defeated those of King James IV.

SDLP: Social Democratic and Labour Party, the largest nationalist party in the North of Ireland.

Sinn Féin: the political party associated with the Republican Movement, the second largest party representing nationalist voters in the North; organises throughout the island of Ireland.

St. John the Baptist Church (St John's) (Chapel): the local Catholic church.

Tour of the North: a parade by the Apprentice Boys – a separate Loyal Order from the Orange Order. It takes place every two years and winds its way through and around various nationalist areas in North Belfast.

Wellworths: major shopping outlet in Portadown.

The Garvaghy Area, July 1998

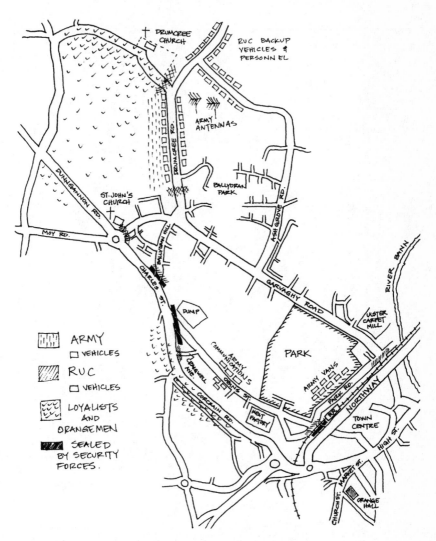

Courtesy: PeaceWatch Ireland

PART I

TESTIMONIES FROM THE
GARVAGHY ROAD

1

Drumcree 1998

Events began to unfold following the decision of the Parades Commission, given on Monday 29th June, that there would not be an Orange parade down the Garvaghy Road on the following Sunday. The community can scarcely be blamed if the news was received with a certain cynicism.

The history of the past three years would not inspire confidence in government promises. For many, it was only when they saw the disorder at Drumcree that they began to believe the Commission's decision. Despite our concerns and misgivings, we had to continue with our preparations to receive and house the international observers, foreign government officials and other high profile guests. We also had to recruit and train our stewards and, in this regard, language is inadequate to render proper thanks to our volunteers for the magnificent job they performed over the trying period.

From the Friday after the Parades Commission's decision, the military started to move in and commenced laying out defence works, mostly barbed wire entanglements; but in the immediate vicinity of Drumcree, a wide-open ditch was opened up. We can say, however, that the siege of Garvaghy Road started on Saturday when we found the road blocked off at St. John's and at the railway bridge at the town end of the road. Further road blockades were to be found at the Tunnel Bridge, Craigwell Avenue and at the foot of Ballyoran Hill, with a barrier across Obins Street, at what was the old Corcrain school.

There was little sleep for anyone on the Saturday night. The Drumcree Community Centre was a constant hive of activity. However, all attention and comment was focused on the actual march which was to leave the town centre at mid-morning. At various vantage points on the route, residents congregated to view the march, with the largest crowd in the vicinity of St. John's Church. Whatever the motives of those taking part, they did little credit to their religion with their offensive taunts concerning the most recent victims of loyalist violence from this community.

Sunday was, all in all, reasonably quiet, even though there was a considerable increase in the numbers gathered about Drumcree following the service and the abortive march 'to the wire!'. Not quite rivaling the Orange hordes, the international media arrived, with their large vehicles taking up prominent position on the Drumcree Road, from which they descended on the unsuspecting residents, ever seeking interviews.

By Monday, the tented village had begun to appear about Drumcree, as well as catering services provided by the numerous chip vans. Not so obvious, but nevertheless present, were the copious supplies of alcohol to fuel the courage of those who sought to fight their way through to the Garvaghy Road. As darkness approached, residents were disturbed both by the roar of the mob and the sound of the low-flying helicopters. An American observer, a one-time colonel in the American Army, said it was a very forcible reminder to him of Vietnam.

On Tuesday morning, I recall, that after only an hour in bed, I got a phone call to go up to St. John's school, where a group of children were awaiting a minibus to bring them to Belfast on route to Dublin Airport and thence to America. The minibus was garaged in Drumcree College, to which all access was barred by an Orange mob gathered around the Dungannon Road roundabout. Following representations by myself and others, the police finally agreed to call in a DMS unit who successfully pushed the mob up the Dungannon Road in the Drumcree direction. The children were then ferried out in four cars which made a hasty beeline for the M1.

The mobs now evolved a tactic of congregating at the various entrances to the besieged area, making it impossible for people to go to work or do shopping or any other urgent business outside the barricades. In the late afternoon, two people had to be rescued from one business premises by a police landrover rather than have them run the gauntlet of the mob. Both filling stations on the Dungannon Road were attacked and subsequently closed. Various suppliers refused to enter the Garvaghy Road, presumably for fear of victimisation at a later date. At this stage, let it be said that it was to the credit of the people and local shopkeepers that all important supplies were maintained.

Tuesday night saw a sharp rise in temperature among the besiegers with both petrol bombs and blast bombs being thrown at the security forces, who replied with plastic baton rounds. From this point on, both the international observers and our own stewards rose magnificently to the occasion, maintaining a twenty-four hour watch and being instrumental in summoning both the councillors and such Assembly Members as were present to incidents where residents were subjected to heavy-handed police tactics. Our representatives made it plain to the security forces that any harassment of their constituents was totally unacceptable and would not be tolerated.

Wednesday afternoon saw an escalation in mob activity, which raised problems for those who had got out to work that morning. Many Catholic families living outside the barbed wire barricades were terrified and either fled the town or sought refuge within the nationalist enclave. Representations had to be continually made regarding the safety of residents of an old people's home and of an isolated nationalist estate. Wednesday saw the arrival of the first food convoy when our friends in Lurgan showed their support and solidarity in a practical manner.

That evening brought a visit from Mr Seamus Mallon, the newly elected Deputy First Minister of the Assembly. Talks with the members of the Coalition brought no change to the situation. Leaving the talks' venue, Mr Mallon was heckled by local residents because of a rumour that he was there to make a deal behind the residents' backs.

On Wednesday evening, loyalist bands led mobs out to Drumcree in a series of illegal processions intended to intimidate nationalists. Thursday morning brought a number of attacks on residents who had ventured 'beyond the wire'. Reports came in about gunfire in other parts of the town. There was a continued build-up of the numbers present at Drumcree, estimated conservatively at around 25,000, with the Orange leadership threatening to make it 100,000 by the 12th of July. That evening produced an escalation in violence characterised by petrol bombs, blast bombs and finally a breaching of the barricades at Drumcree. This caused considerable apprehension and fear, especially to the residents of Ashley Heights, who, recalling a similar break-through in 1996, began to consider the possibility of evacuation, even though they were within the 'ring of steel'.

That night saw numerous arrests of Orange followers and serious casualties among the security forces. A food convoy from Belfast was expected on Friday. Reports from observers indicated a lessening of activity on the part of the Orange mobs, but this proved of little comfort as the security forces initiated a particularly intensive search of the convoy. The search, it was believed, was intended to facilitate an Orange assault which did succeed in attacking the vehicles at the tail of the convoy. This searching was in marked contrast to the uninterrupted free passage of loyalist vehicles with their supplies of blast bombs and booze to Drumcree.

On Friday, contact was made by the British government regarding proximity talks aimed at resolving the situation. The talks were scheduled for Saturday 11th July. It was Friday night that the violence at Drumcree took a new turn, when gunmen attacked the security forces. Though some loyalist rioters were arrested, the gunman got away among the throng of Orangemen. The shooting, the continued detonation of blast bombs and the noise of three helicopters created an atmosphere of extreme tension within the nationalist population. Sleep in such circumstances, was definitely a luxury.

By Saturday the possibility of talks was the main concern. These were scheduled to start at 9.00am, but problems regarding the venue delayed proceedings; so it was not until 3.00pm that the talks commenced at Armagh District Council offices. Despite an all-round commitment not to breach confidentiality, the Orange Order, by way of Denis Watson, gave a radio interview during the talks, and this, along with the application to the Parades Commission to march on the Garvaghy Road at 12.30pm on Sunday, indicate that good faith was confined solely to members of the Coalition.

The application to march, timed as it was, caused great apprehension among residents, who believed they had been sold out. To reassure people, Breandán Mac Cionnaith called a meeting, at which he made it clear that the original Parades Commission decision would not be overturned and that there would be no march in the morning. The crowd at Drumcree was somewhat smaller on Saturday night, presumably in the expectation that they would have their march on Sunday, and for the same reason, presumably, there was considerably less violence. Whatever trouble did arise was alcohol related.

Sunday morning brought the tragic news of the Quinn children and evoked a deep and sympathetic response among residents, who had no hesitation in laying the guilt firmly on the Orange Order. The plea from Rev. Bingham, the County Chaplain, that the protest should end showed that at least one Orangeman had a conscience. A festival planned for the local children that day was cancelled as a mark of respect for the innocent victims of Orange terrorism. The number of protesters on Sunday evening was considerably diminished, possibly due to the events of that day.

On Monday, despite major Orange demonstrations taking place in Lurgan and Gilford, both within a short distance of Portadown, the promise of 100,000 Orangemen at Drumcree did not materialise. Not more than a couple of thousand turned up and these were addressed by those well-known Christian pacifists Ian Paisley, William McCrea and Paul Berry! None of these, doubtlessly, had anything to do with the gas cylinder bombs that had exploded against the security barrier at Drumcree that night.

The sham fight at Scarva took place on Tuesday (14th July). This led us to believe that there would be an even larger gathering at Drumcree, where the atmosphere would be intensified by the presence of Scottish bands. These bands did eventually appear, and were led by several gentlemen who vigorously urged the bands forward to march along the Dungannon Road to Drumcree. This, of course, was another illegal march, fully observed by the RUC, who doubtlessly will be bringing prosecutions against those responsible! Tuesday night's demonstration was, if anything, louder than anything before, enhanced by the playing of the Scottish bands, not to mention the noise of the inevitable helicopters. However, it turned out this was the 'Last Hurrah'.

On Wednesday, we were wakened with the news that the RUC and British army had at long last moved into the fields beyond the wires and across the trenches, to conduct a prolonged search of the whole area. This led to a mob gathering on the Dungannon Road, where entry back to the vicinity of the church was prevented. The mob dispersed in the early hours of Thursday.

The security forces continued their search of the fields around Drumcree Church on Thursday, finding blast bombs, a machine gun and other weaponry. Some Orange officials were permitted as far as the church to continue their protest and David Jones laughably claimed the weapons were planted by republicans! An Orange rally was called on Friday night, with an expected attendance of 15,000. Crowds, now dwindling to perhaps a few hundred, continued to move up and down the Dungannon Road.

On Friday, the last food convoy arrived from Derry. The drivers were given an escorted tour of the 'fortification' at the different points of the area. The Coalition, which had been in what amounted to almost continuous session throughout the 'emergency', called for yet another meeting at this time to confirm that the proximity talks were to resume the next day in

Armagh. The Orange rally, scheduled for Friday night, once again necessitated our stewards and observers patrolling the area throughout the night. Despite expectations of the organisers, the rally turned out to be very disappointing, with an attendance variously calculated at between 1,000 – 2,000, and their placards indicated that many had been bussed in. A number of Orange supporters continued their attempts to return to Drumcree, but their efforts were frustrated by the security forces, who would permit only a token Orange presence there.

Saturday morning at 8.00am, the designated representatives of the Coalition assembled at the Drumcree Centre in preparation for the resumption of the proximity talks in Armagh. The talks began at 9.00am and finished at midnight. Once again, no progress was made on resolving the crisis.

Early on Sunday morning the security forces commenced dismantling their defences.

The above is but a brief summary of the events which took place over a period of fourteen days in July 1998. It shows that whatever fears and apprehension we felt as individuals, as a community we displayed the best qualities of calmness and discipline in the face of adversity. This is equally true of the youth of both sexes who behaved in a dignified manner throughout.

Anyone who has ever questioned the activities of the Garvaghy Road Residents' Coalition in opposing Orange parades should reflect on the gross behaviour of the hostile hordes who gathered at Drumcree Church under the banner of Portadown District LOL No. 1, and they will be convinced of the correctness of our stance.

Joe

2

No one said it was going to be easy

We had gathered in the Drumcree Centre, Coalition and residents alike, smoking, chatting and drinking tea in anticipation of the arrival of the Parades Commission's hand delivered envelope. The North of Ireland was holding its breath, all waiting for the decision, but no one more than us, because we eat, sleep and breathe the road every day of the year.

With every new arrival, the words, 'Any news?", was always the greeting. The answer being 'No', they inevitably would decide to stay and join the rest of the hopefuls, the doubters, and the 'don't know brigade'.

Lost in my own thoughts, I didn't see the man enter. Then my name was called; I was ushered into a room and watched as the two large brown envelopes were produced. Every eye in the room was on them. I wanted them opened yet was too afraid to look in case the decision went against us. Like a kick to the heart, I knew it could be 'fatal' (what a word to use but then this is Portadown where people have died that Orangemen might march Garvaghy Road).

In the seconds that followed, faces could be read. Have we done enough? Enough talking on behalf of our community; the Irish government, British government, Parades Commission, and other interested bodies every time telling us that we have right on our side? Trying to explain what it is like to live on the Garvaghy Road, what it is like living in Portadown, what little we have but more importantly what we don't! How will the community react to a 'yeah' or 'nay'? Could I sit on the road again? Have hopes been dashed like so many times before? Was this going to be the year when the residents would not stand alone?

The envelopes were opened and we crowded around. Some could be heard praying; others searched the booklet that would tell us our fate. Pages were turned and mumbled reading could be heard; the agonizing search for the decision bore fruit on the back pages. What a relief: they had been re-routed. At the same time, Alistair Graham from the Parades Commission could be heard reading the decision on a specially extended news bulletin on the radio in the next room. A loud cheer went up from the residents.

As I came out of the room, I met a lot of 'Didn't I tell you so? I knew all along' people. Others thanking God, some looked relieved, others had smiles like Cheshire cats. To me it was the start of a community coming together and I was to witness a lot of this during the coming weeks.

The Coalition had rented a room in the centre; we had installed everything we needed, a desk, telephones, filing system, computer, and if two or more people were to enter the room, it was full. A rota had to be worked out whereby the phones and faxes had to be answered and the organizing of our guests worked out. We had international observers from America, Canada, South Africa, England, and nationalists from North and South were all due to arrive on Friday and Saturday. They all had to be placed in homes before the big day, Sunday.

From Monday, when we received the word, until the Friday, felt like a month. I was lucky that I was saying good-bye to my youngest son Barry. He was being brought on holiday to the Free State by my friend, Eileen. We felt that at his tender age he had witnessed too much over the last few years.

Saturday 4th July started early with the arrival of the international observers. Most had been staying in Belfast for a few days, but they – all 81 of them – made their way here that day. Earlier that day my first visitor had arrived, a local man from the Dungannon Road. I feared that he would be attacked and persuaded him to stay with me. His knowledge and words of wisdom had a calming effect on me and those who stayed at my house.

From 2.00pm onward our visitors arrived and we sorted them into different houses. The problem we had was that we had a lot more foreign visitors than the previous year and those residents who did take them last year wanted nationalists instead. Houses were running out all too fast. I had images of judges, solicitors, senators and an ambassador having to share a tent if something drastic wasn't done. With my powers of persuasion, sometimes downright abuse, people started taking people into their homes. Some had been here the year before so they tended to keep the others in check. Belfast and Derry people started to arrive and they were quickly given a cup of tea, something to eat and told to make themselves at home until people arrived to house them. We also had visitors from Tipperary, Galway, Dublin and Kerry.

Saturday night was very tense and the centre was full to overflowing. People had organised themselves into different groups. Some were making tea and sandwiches, others putting their names forward to steward the area. Mobile phones and walkie-talkies had been obtained and were being carried by people, so as to relay messages from Obins Street and different parts of the Garvaghy Road. Nothing was left to chance; we wouldn't be caught out like '97.

My visitor himself had visitors, two gentlemen who talked into the early hours of the morning. Although both were men with good standing in the community, I was wondering what the gossip mongers were thinking on Sunday morning when we all left the house to go and watch the parade pass St John's chapel.

We stood, residents, international observers, nationalists from North and South, together, behind rolls of barbed wire, while dark-suited, sash-wearing men walked past us by the thousand. It all brought back unhappy memories of July 1997. I connect Orangemen with pain, blood, anger, frustration and a feeling of hopelessness. I hoped and prayed that they would hand in a letter of protest and go home. But watching their followers shouting abuse, I knew it wouldn't happen. Those not familiar with the area stood open-mouthed and staring. As it was pointed out to them from where we stood, those that had already passed us could be seen entering the Church grounds, and still row after row of well-dressed bigots passed us. Twenty thousand, it said there would be. The media reckoned they numbered between 5,000-7,000.

It was decided that the phones had to be 'manned' day and night, so my turn came on Monday midnight to 7.00am. During the night I got a lot of visitors in the office, the craic was great and the stories hilarious. At 3.00am some stewards returned to catch up on lost sleep. The lights were dimmed and an eerie silence descended in the office. Between the hours of four o'clock and six o'clock in the morning, which I called the twilight zone, I felt as if I was the only one in the world awake. Seven o'clock couldn't come quickly enough. At 6.45am, just as I could feel my eyes closing, a man entered the office to report that the Project Children group due to fly to America that day couldn't get to their minibus as Orangemen had decided to block the road. It soon emerged that the Tunnel bridge and Shillington's bridge were also blocked and people couldn't get to work.

After a few phone calls, making sure our two councillors Joe and Breandán knew the situation, I along with a few others made our way up to the St. John's Church.

Joe and I approached the police and explained the situation, how the children had to be in Belfast airport at 8.00am and the time was now 6.55am Gerald Cusack got three children into his car and an international observer and two other men did likewise. I feared the men would be attacked on their return journey alone and, after asking some parents to accompany them, I along with another friend jumped into the cars and we drove at speed through the Orangemen whom the police were gently pushing back. The children in the car never uttered a word.

Through all the ups and downs I experienced during the days of Drumcree, one memory will stick with me of a wee girl being sick out an open window, crying, looking to go home as we sped down the motorway on the start of what should have been a holiday of a lifetime. All four cars arrived safely in Belfast and the organisers of Project Children, who had been contacted earlier about the situation, worked quickly, sorting out the children, and before too long we were waving them goodbye as their bus pulled out. Returning to Portadown the Orangemen were pushed back at Shillington's and we arrived back safe and sound.

A family who had gone on holiday and had given me the key to their home were due to arrive home later that day. Any international observers I had staying there had to be moved. Most were easy to sort out except one who was sick. I knew he couldn't go up and down stairs and he needed a bungalow. I took him into our house, but had to explain that my house was full and he would be lucky to get a bed. We had a total of seven people in the house. Luckily, I had borrowed a friend's caravan, so some had to move in there.

Lurgan was the first of the food convoys to arrive. People and a local priest had organised a food collection going from house to house. Food, nappies, toiletries, cups, napkins were all brought, one community helping another! Slagging and banter was tossed from groups of workmates. The Lurgan ones were saying that times had changed when Lurgan was feeding Portadown people, and better still, the Portadown ones were accepting it! Veteran republican comrades J B O'Hagan and Ned Tennyson embraced one another at the door. Being handed a cup of tea and sandwiches, they found themselves a quiet corner to reminisce about old times.

Young and old alike coming together, all doing their bit! Barry Watson, community activist, took his seat at the front door! His unique armband with his name on it could be seen from a mile away. He said he was there to do his bit. He did more, refusing to go home for his tea. If he was to be paid for his effort, we wouldn't have enough to pay him.

The Belfast and Derry convoys came next. Parcels were handed from one person to another. So much was given that St Mary's Hall had to be opened to hold it all. Every town seemed to be sending something. The phones were busy with messages of support, the fax machine working hard as page after page of messages arrived. Sometimes we got nasty phone calls, one which left me speechless. The vile and obscene messages being spewed from the mouths of men and women, young and old threatened not only members of the Coalition, but the entire community.

On a few nights I took myself up to the Drumcree Road to see what was going on. Different international observers who were allowed over to the other side of the barbed wire could tell us what was happening, how many Orangemen had gathered, what the military were doing, how many plastic bullets had been fired.

One day drifted into another, all basically the same, except when we had meetings with the Irish government, Seamus Mallon, Sean Neeson, Monica McWilliams, Martin McGuinness and Gerry Adams. They were all supportive.

During the two weeks of the siege, I can honestly say I was proud to be a member of this community. People were coming together, be it by taking people into their homes, making sandwiches, tea, giving out food parcels, checking on the elderly, lifting prescriptions, or minding other people's children. Those that were not a part of it all really lost out. But if I were to pick one group that I felt had done the most it must be the stewards – our locals, nationalists and international observers – who patrolled our streets day and night in all weathers! We owe them a debt this community could never repay.

As our visitors started to depart from my house it all came back to normality. Myself and my children, who had played their part stewarding, sat down to a good dinner after which we all retired to bed to try and catch up on our lost sleep.

My final thoughts on these few weeks are: 'what a waste!' Two lost weeks taken out of our lives, and a waste of money on security, when our hospitals need so much. Finally, but more importantly, what a waste of three young lives when the Quinn brothers were burnt to death in their beds! We all have a share, a portion of blame, myself included. As a mother of three children, I will have to learn to live with that. No-one said it was going to be easy. Such a high price for our rights!

Donna

3

Under Siege

Monday 29th June

I have decided to keep a diary from today, through the events of Drumcree whatever happens. Today the Parades Commission made its decision on the Drumcree parade. I was unable to hear the radio from where I was, so at 11 o'clock I asked Maurice had he heard the decision. He told me the parade's homeward leg was re-routed. Even though I am against the Orange march, which I feel is sectarian and triumphalist, my heart skipped a beat and my blood ran cold. I know the Portadown Orange will not agree to re-route in a peaceful way.

When I got home this afternoon the phone never stopped ringing. Everyone heard the news and although they are all happy that at last we nationalists seemed to be getting a fair share, we are all very afraid.

Almost everyone in work has stopped talking to me. If this is how they behave and it is still days to the parade, what will it be like later? Three girls, two of whom I always sit with at lunch, changed their lunch time without telling me, so I was left sitting in the canteen on my own. It feels awful.

Tuesday 30 June

Still no one talking to me today. They keep giving me dirty looks. The girls are taking different breaks again. Maybe it's best if I just keep my head down and not say too much. They might leave me alone. A couple of guys in work said they will

16

walk the Garvaghy Road. I said you probably will. I walked away from them thinking, 'I hope you don't, you Orange bigots'.

When I got home, everyone was saying the police and army were measuring the roads along the Garvaghy Road all day. There is fear that they are going to do a U-turn and let them down. Tony Blair, Bertie Ahern, Mo Mowlam and Ronnie Flanagan have all said they will stand firm to uphold the rule of law. Well, here's hoping they mean it. If they do, it will be the first time.

Wednesday 1 July

The supporters of the Orangemen burned ten Catholic chapels last night. My God, how can these people hope to win when they have lost even the fear of God? I hope our side won't burn churches in retaliation. We need God on our side.

I don't trust the RUC to hold the line. The RUC are known as the military wing of the Orange Order in nationalist areas so we don't have much faith in their ability or desire to stand up against the Orangemen.

Still no one really talking to me. About eight guys were sitting in the smoke room at work. When I looked up they were staring at me with hate-filled eyes. I went bright red and nearly fell over my own feet trying to get to the back of the machine where they couldn't see me so clearly. The dirty looks and no one talking to me – it's starting to get me down. At 9.30am I went home. I told our team leader, I was going home. She asked, 'Has anyone said anything to you?' I said, 'No, that's the problem.' They must be talking if she asked me that straight away.

I went and did my shopping. We have been advised to get plenty of food in, so my cupboards and fridge are full.

Thursday 2nd July

I went to work today. There are a few Catholics in the place I work, but they would number only about six or seven of more than 100 employees. Two of them came over and said they were glad I had come back. They told me not to let the 'Prods' drive me out. I don't know if I am strong enough. I am the only

Catholic in my section, so I am alone. I was working on my own today doing another job, thank God. Today was a very long day and I was very happy to see three o'clock. I was so wound up and nervous today, I came home and fell asleep.

The Orange Order still won't talk to us; they have been very quiet. There is talk that if they don't get down the road they will turn off the electricity and water. Everyone is buying candles and saving bottles to store water.

The Women's Peace Camp was set up today, so Michelle and I went along to help. My son had given his tent to be used at the camp. If the police and army run over it like last year, I have sworn to buy him a new one. The spirits of the women at the camp are high and we have a good laugh.

Friday 3rd July

It's my birthday today. I don't feel much like celebrating somehow. Joanne and Lorraine were working with me today. They have chatted away to me all day, which is such a relief. They also said how sorry they were about the chapels being burnt. I almost cried because someone had the courage and good heart to say something. We got to go home at 1.00pm. I don't have to go back for two weeks. Maybe then things will be back to normal.

I have volunteered along with Steve to do some stewarding, so I went to the meeting at 7.30pm. Steve had to go to Dublin to drive some boys to the airport. He took our son Stephen with him. I can't settle until he's back.

I have just been given five American film-makers to keep at my house. I only offered to keep two or three, but I now have five: Claire, Sandy, Eileen, Sheila and Ericka. They want my family to be in their film, so we all agreed. It might be fun and it will take the kids' minds off things.

Residents' meeting in St. Mary's Hall tonight. Rosemary Nelson said at last the law is on our side. Breandán Mac Cionnaith reminded everyone that the community had agreed there would be no drink or trouble towards the police or army. Everyone clapped and cheered. We are a community united, not a puppet of Sinn Féin, as we are so often portrayed. We are now surrounded by a ring of steel.

Saturday 4th July

My sister's birthday today – in all the fuss I forgot to get her a card. I spent last night at the Women's Peace and Justice Camp. The craic was great and spirits are high, but even with all this we still kept looking around at every passing car. I was afraid some madman would shoot up at us. I don't know what the others were thinking and I didn't ask. The Peace Camp was wound up at 12 noon today. Everyone was afraid that we might get a repeat of last year when the police and army used landrovers to turn over the tents at 3.30am, without even looking or asking if anyone was asleep in the tents. Only sheer luck prevented a death.

Steve and I are marshals tonight along with others. We start at 7.00pm, right through until 1pm tomorrow. So I'm off to get some sleep. Every road into and out of this area is blocked off. We are now under siege. If the Orangemen strike medals this year to commemorate the Siege of Drumcree '98, I hope they send us some.

Sunday 5th July

I stayed out until 4am last night. I had to come home. I was falling asleep on my feet and Steve said I should go home, so I did.

Got up again at 8.30am, just as Steve was coming home. Had a shower and went to 10.00am Mass in St. John's. The chapel is surrounded by barbed wire. The sight of it is frightening – and also sad. We, the Garvaghy Road residents will talk to anyone at any time, but the Orange refuses to talk to us. Surely talking would be so much better than this wall of hate to keep us apart.

The Orange Order went to church. I watched them from my bedroom window and I prayed that they would walk home again the same way. But I don't hold out much hope. The

Orangemen came from their service, walked up to the police lines, were refused entrance and the stand-off begins. We are under siege.

Will the police allow them to gather in their thousands tonight until sheer force of numbers allow the police to say they have to let them down the road for public safety?

The dog isn't eating. I wonder if she feels the tension which is so real you can almost see it.

Monday 6th July

Day two of the stand-off. The field behind our house is unprotected. So is the entrance to Garvaghy Park. Breandán Mac Cionnaith and Joe Duffy, our two local councillors, have asked for them to be protected. So far nothing has been done by the police or army. Some of the local men have erected a barricade across the bottom of Garvaghy Park to protect themselves and their area. The police are not amused and want it removed, but they say they will remove it when the police offer some sort of protection to replace it. The police move away and offer nothing, so the barricade remains in place. This doesn't help us as we are still unprotected.

The American girls left for Belfast at 4.00pm. They are coming back later in the week.

I have just stood in my back garden as a huge crowd of Orangemen and their supporters – both walking and in cars – have gone up to join those already at Drumcree. It is dark, but I have all the house lights out. I'm terrified if they make a break for it they will be right in my back garden. Steve's out doing marshall again. I am alone with the boys. Susan is staying with Michelle because Alan is also doing marshal and Michelle wants someone to talk to and keep her company. What will I do if they attack my house? I don't go to bed until 4.00am, when Steve comes home.

Tuesday 7th July

Two helicopters landed 40 feet from my back garden. I was in the kitchen; all I could see was what I thought was black smoke.

I ran out thinking they had come and set my house on fire. Thank God, it was the helicopters landing and sending up a huge cloud of smoke. Around 20 riot police got out of the helicopters and formed a line across the field. A few minutes later, a crowd of around 200 loyalists came up the road with a band, flags and banners. They were shouting and roaring. I thought if they make a break for it, how will 20 police hold them back? I ran inside and locked the door. When they had gone past, the helicopters arrived and took the police away, leaving us again unprotected.

I can't take much more of this. I can't sleep, can't eat; I feel like I am going to have a nervous breakdown. Michelle rang and asked if I would do an interview for GMTV with her. At first I said no, then changed my mind. Martin Frizzell, the interviewer, was very nice. Michelle always liked him, so I think it was more so she could meet him that she agreed to do the interview. I was wanted just so that she could have someone to share the experience with.

Wednesday 8th July

I was up at Drumcree Centre at 11.30am when a food convoy arrived from Lurgan. A local priest had organised it, mainly to show us we are not alone. Lurgan nationalists are with us and are prepared to support us. The food will be given out to old-age pensioners and single parents.

At 8.30pm we gathered to say the Rosary for peace. We said five decades and sang songs. The middle of the room was covered with candles and a special blessed candle was given to us. Sister Laura played an extract from Martin Luther King's 'I Have a Dream' speech. It was very moving when we all joined it at the end with 'We Shall Overcome'. I cried because I was so proud of the ordinary people in that room. When I looked around, my tears were not the only ones flowing. My batteries were recharged. To come from the peace and safety of that room into the tension on the streets was unbelievable.

Steve on marshal duty again tonight. I wish he would stay home, but I know it is something he feels he has to do, not just for us but for everyone in the area. I am so proud of him. He needs to get some rest; he looks exhausted. I know he won't stop, so I say nothing and smile when I see him. There's no point wasting the time we do get together fighting.

Thursday 9th July

Sheila, one of the Americans, came back this morning. I gave her something to eat and she went out to see what was happening. The local radio station, Radio Equality, is coming through loud and clear. It is a pirate station, set up to keep us informed as to what is going on. Local people are doing DJ, so we aren't expecting great music and quality reports, but it is good to listen to. Best of all, it stops you going crazy wondering what's going on.

Tonight 15,000 Orangemen and their supporters have gathered at Drumcree. Are the police mad to let this number gather? They are now firing blast bombs and petrol bombs, and ball bearings from high-powered catapults at the police. The TV is telling us there are injured security forces and loyalists.

The huge bangs and flashes are fireworks. I can hear them and see them light up the sky. The police have started to fire baton rounds at them. The back of my house is still unprotected. I'm terrified; Steve's out again. The boys and I sit in the dark, afraid to turn on the lights in case we bring attention to the house. The noise and flashes have become too much. I get Steve's shotgun. God forgive me, but if they come with petrol bombs to burn my house or hurt my kids, I'll shoot them.

Friday 10th July

Monica McWilliams came today. She was on the local radio. She didn't know it was illegal. I spoke to her and asked her some questions. I told her of our fears and asked why the RUC and army were letting them gather in their thousands. She is going to see Ronnie Flanagan and put those questions to him.

At 12.30pm a huge convoy arrived from Belfast with food and toys. The police held up the convoy and began to search every car. Why are they searching these cars, which are all clearly marked, and yet allowing thousands of loyalists and Orangemen to go to Drumcree unhindered – carrying blast and petrol bombs and goodness knows what else?

The police finally allow the convoy to continue. They have taken two hammers, a car wheel brace, a pocket key-ring penknife and a toy baseball bat from some of the cars. They show them to the media, Breandán Mac Cionnaith and Rosemary Nelson as weapons which have been seized! Even the media are laughing. While the convoy was stopped some loyalists attacked the back few cars; windows were smashed by stone throwers. A woman and a man both had cuts on their legs and a few others have bruises. Nothing more serious, thank God.

Good news! The Orange Order have agreed to proximity talks with Breandán and the Coalition tomorrow, starting at 9.00am. We all hope something is sorted out, but we don't trust their (Orange) motives. Why do they want to talk now after all this time? – after calling us monsters who should be locked in cages (David McNarry on 'UTV Live').

Tonight Orangemen and loyalists are rioting with police at Drumcree again. Live gun rounds and blast and petrol bombs again targeted at police. Twenty loyalists and four policemen are injured. I have no sympathy for rioters, but I can see how the police are doing their best and my heart is beginning to hurt for them and their families.

Michelle and I wandered around until 11.00pm. The noise and flashes, the shouts of anger and cheers coming from Drumcree can be heard on the Garvaghy Road. It's like psychological warfare. It's starting to wear me down; not only me – the kids and Steve and everyone else on the road. Why don't they stop? Please make them go away! Am I starting to lose my mind? Is this what lack of sleep and this almighty fear and tension does to people? Steve is out marshalling again. He came back to see if we were ok at about 1am. I was in such a state, he showed me how to load his shotgun, but stayed with me until I fell asleep, fully clothed on top of the bed. Then he slipped out to marshal all night.

Saturday 11th July

Talks between the two sides didn't start until 3.00pm. They couldn't agree on a venue, so agreeing on anything else looks very unlikely. One loyalist rioter shot by a plastic bullet is very ill. I have prayed he is alright. Nothing is worth even one human life being lost. I have also prayed for the police and Brits and their families. Please God intervene and solve this with dignity and justice for both sides.

They have a new mural at Churchill. It looks great. It's like a copy of the Agreement document, but with three Irish dancers and over it all is bending one Orangeman holding a petrol bomb with red, white and blue flames coming out of it.

I knew the Orange Order were up to something while the Residents' Coalition were having talks with them in Armagh. The Orange Order have applied for a new march tomorrow which comes from Drumcree Church, down the Garvaghy Road. So much for the good faith of the Orange Order! Can we ever trust them? The Parades Commission are staying up all night to decide if they will allow this march. I don't understand why they are even going to consider this new application. It's the same march; the Orange haven't given the 28 days' notice required, and they are still sitting up there at Drumcree breaking the law!

The area is very fearful. Is this how the British government are going to get them down the road? Are we to be broken again? Is our community again to be raped by the almighty Orange Order? Please God let this be ok! Have we suffered six days of hell for nothing? Have the croppies been beaten down again?

I hate them. I hate them. I hate them for making me hide in my home in the dark, too afraid to turn on the lights. I hate them for making my children hide in the dark. I hate them for calling us monsters and not human beings. I hate them for making me think of murder. I hate them for making me hate them. I'm not sorry. I hate them and I don't care if God forgives me!

They are fighting hand to hand with them at Drumcree. Residents' meeting at 11.00 p.m tonight. Breandán told us he had put across the idea of a Forum where the representatives of everybody affected by Drumcree could discuss the sectarianism and discrimination in the town. He said the British government suggested there was £15 million on offer if a solution could be reached. The Orange Order's effort at compromise was to suggest they either marched the Garvaghy Road or Obins Street. Both were rejected. They all came away with no agreement.

God help us! The Parades Commission can't reverse the decision and allow them down – can they?

Sunday 12th July

I wake up to the terrible news that three wee boys – Jason, Mark and Richard Quinn, aged 10, 9 and 7, all brothers – have been burned to death in their home in Ballymoney. The police have said it was a 'purely sectarian attack'. Madmen have come in the middle of the night and with their hearts filled with hate and their eyes blinded by evil, they threw a petrol bomb and murdered three innocent children. I wonder if those monsters who did this knew they would murder children. I refuse to think that human beings could knowingly do this.

The Reverend Ian Paisley told us earlier this week to use our imagination as to what could happen if the Orange Order did not walk the Garvaghy Road before 12th July. This terrible evil thing was done in his constituency. Did his words inflame their evil hearts? The Rev. Ian Paisley, David McNarry and others should be indicted under the Incitement to Hatred Act. Of course they won't be.

I have to stop writing for a while, because I can't even see the page for tears. Oh God, help their poor mother!

The Parades Commission have rejected the Orange Order's request for a new parade. I suppose they could have done nothing else. The waiting for their decision gave us something else to fear, something else to eat away at the hope and courage which keeps us going.

Oh God, I can't get those children out of my mind. My son Andrew is sitting clutching his Barney Bear. He has packed his toy computer into his bag and has left it beside the front door. I haven't let him know about those wee boys. I ask him why?

He said, 'if the Orangemen come, mummy, I have Barney and I will run away with my computer.' My God, how can I help my son? He is only ten; one of those wee boys was ten. I go into the bathroom. I sit in the corner on the floor and cry quietly so he can't hear me.

The Devil must be laughing at the evil now done in God's name. How will the Orange distance themselves from this?

I went to 10 o'clock Mass. Bishop Sean Brady was giving the sermon. I lit a candle for those wee boys. I know God will welcome them into Heaven with open arms.

David Trimble has at last asked the Orange Order to go home. The Rev. William Bingham has also asked them to go home. Ronnie Flanagan said this is murder, not protest. The Portadown Orangemen have voted unanimously to remain. They said the boys' deaths had nothing to do with them!

Monday 13th July

Last night was very quiet. No fireworks, no gunfire, no petrol bombs, no blast bombs, no baton rounds, no cheers and no helicopters or drums. Police reports said there were very few up at Drumcree. Have the Orange Order realised at last what they have done? Steve spent the first night since Saturday 4th July in his own bed. I thank God he has at last got some sleep.

The Orange march down the Ormeau Road in Belfast passed off peacefully. The residents tried to get the court to overturn the Parades Commission decision to allow the march, but lost. They held a silent black flag protest while the Orangemen marched by.

I spoke to a few people about letting the Orange Order down the Garvaghy Road and also holding a black flag protest. We talked it through and we realised that if we give in this time, these madmen will think every time they want Catholics to give in, they only have to murder our children. We felt we would be signing our children's death warrants. We must stand firm.

The strength of character those on the Ormeau Road showed today was wonderful. Please God, let me have some of that courage and strength if I need it. Take some of the hate and anger out of my heart.

Tuesday 14th July

Clare and Sheila, whose dad is very ill, are going home to America today. They both hope to come back, to do some more work here. I will miss them; they kept the kids and me busy. Sandy, another of the Americans also left. She is going down to County Wicklow to try and trace her ancestors. She has her great, great, grandmother's birth certificate.

Orla rang and is trying to get a meeting of the DFJ organised. Everyone in the area got some food from the convoy. It was a good morale booster.

Two men were arrested for the murder of the wee Quinn brothers. I hope they are the ones, so the family will get some justice.

David Jones, the Portadown Orange spokesman is trying to sell some story about drug involvement in the boys' murder. The Orange Order never stop sinking to the lowest depths! After trying to wash their hands of these murders, they dare try to sully the name of the wee dead boys and their family! The RUC have completely denied this and have called for an end to these terrible rumours.

I think I am losing my mind. I can't eat, sleep or even tidy the house. I just watch the news, smoke and wonder what is going to happen next. I shout at the kids, then I say sorry and disappear for a wee cry.

The security forces have finally put some barbed wire across the field behind us, so I feel a bit more secure.

Steve's still out at night, but it's a whole lot quieter. I took a sleeping pill someone gave me and went to bed at 1.30am.

Wednesday 15th July

Gerry Adams came to see us today. He said the dignity and courage we had shown on the Garvaghy Road was an inspiration to nationalists throughout Ireland.

He and Breandán went for a walk through the area. I have met him three times now and each time I am struck by the very calm, honest and genuine man he is. I hope he can keep his people on the path of peace.

Some of the food which was sent in to us is being given to Michael McGoldrick to take out to the children in Romania. Steve went to give him a hand to load it on to the lorry he had brought. Some of the food is also being given to a local man who brings workers out to Romania each year. They have to bring their own food, so this will help him in his good work.

Giving away some of the food is also a healing thing for our own community. We feel that even in the depths of our own despair and pain we can still think of and have the goodness of heart to help others who we know are also suffering.

Some of us in the DFJ are trying to organise a healing mass in our community. I have to see Father Gerry and Father Michael about the mass tomorrow, maybe try to get the children involved and also organise some music. Father Gerry proved he can play the guitar at the recent Rosary for Peace night.

The police and army have gone in and cleared Drumcree Church and grounds. They are conducting a search. So far, they have found several blast bombs, masks, catapults, nuts and bolts. They have also found a homemade machine gun and ammunition. It sort of puts the Orange Order's idea of peaceful protest up for question. So far, twenty have been arrested up at Drumcree. Amongst them is a leading 'loyalist rights' person: Pauline Gilmore. I wonder was she defending her right to attack the security forces and create mayhem!

More people have been arrested in connection with the murder of those three wee Quinn boys. The Orange Order has given up the suggestion of drug involvement. Now it says the RUC were in some way involved. Those people (Orange) are getting so desperate, they are even trying to blacken the memory of dead children.

Thursday 16th July

David Jones was on TV today giving off about the police and army not letting them into the field at Drumcree. The Church of Ireland has told the protesters at Drumcree to move off church land and has locked the gates to prevent them from gathering there anymore. I suppose petrol and blast bombs, shooting at the security forces, riots and mayhem are not the sort of thing the Church of Ireland wants to see on its consecrated ground. The Orange Order has been evicted and the stand-off is becoming more and more ridiculous. Why don't they just pick up what dignity they may still have and go home? 500 British troops have flown home, so the government must think the situation is calming down.

Meanwhile, we here on the Garvaghy Road are still surrounded by barricades and security forces. Paratroopers walked through my garden today. The sight of them makes my blood run cold.

I rang Father Michael. He said I would need to speak to Father Gerry and the Parish Council about the healing mass. Gerry is away until Monday. Lucky Gerry; I wish I could go away for a few days!

Friday 17th July

Pauline Gilmore has been charged with terrorist offences. My son went to his wee student job today. I went to town for the first time in almost two weeks. No one said anything, but I was very nervous. The Portadown Orange have called for a mass rally in town tonight. Haven't they learned what happens when they throw out those wild calls? Maybe they have learned, but just don't care anymore.

I'm sitting in my kitchen. It's almost 10.00pm and I can hear the sound of many car horns blaring, just over the houses. The sound is frightening. My nerves are in tatters. What will they do tonight? I heard they are going to light their bonfires tonight. They had said they wouldn't light them until the Orangemen marched the Garvaghy Road. I suppose they have given up on that idea and have decided to light them before the woodworm has a feast and there was nothing left to burn.

It's 10.30pm now and they have just lit the bonfire at the back of Obins Street. The horns are still blaring, they have started shouting and the riot police have pulled up into the field behind my house and are stopping cars coming from the Drumcree direction. If I had the grip of David Jones now I wouldn't be responsible for my actions. He calls those madmen onto the streets and sits back to watch the fear they cause. Another night sitting in my home in the dark. Oh God, how many more?

Steve and I went up to Susan's bedroom and opened the side window. We could see the bonfire. The flames danced into the air, lighting up the night sky. It was strangely beautiful. We could hear the wood crackling and the shouts and cheers of the crowd. I wonder what they would have said if they knew two Garvaghy Road Catholics were enjoying their bonfire almost as much as they were, even if for different reasons. In spite of the bonfire or maybe because of it, everything seems quiet up at Drumcree.

Earlier today it was revealed that the Rev. William Bingham and some other ministers who had asked the Orangemen to go home from Drumcree had received death threats.

Saturday 18th July

It's my niece's birthday today. I forgot her card; will bring it up later. My memory is getting worse.

Today I have written two letters of protest to the *Portadown Times* and the *Belfast Telegraph*.

The protest rally the Orangemen called for last night was a bit of a disaster for them. Over 2,000 turned up, even though there are over 1,200 Orange Order members in Portadown alone. Maybe this is showing how the vast numbers of Orangemen feel about the Drumcree stand-off. I hope so. Even though things seem to be a bit more calm, I am still very nervous and uptight. I keep getting headaches and still can't sleep properly. When I went to bed tonight all was quiet. There are reports that many Portadown Orangemen are going to resign over the handling of Drumcree.

Sunday 19th July

I woke up this morning to find the barbed wire which was defending the field behind my house was gone. In the middle of the night the army had dismantled all the security fences around the Garvaghy Road. Those at Obins Street and Craigwell Avenue have also been taken down. We are completely defenceless now. I wonder how long it will take some loyalist madman to carry out an attack. The people of this area were not informed of the security scale down and we are afraid. The police and army have said that regular foot patrols will cover the area. How long until even they are gone?

Three Protestant ministers have resigned from the Orange Order. A spokesman said others are set to follow. Have they seen that the Orange Order has lost all claim to being a Christian organisation? The Orange and the Residents' spokespeople met in Armagh again today for proximity talks. These talks broke up again after fifteen hours with no agreement.

I go back to work tomorrow. I hope they leave me alone. I hope I get news of another job soon. I don't know how long I will be able to stand it if they don't talk to me and keep giving me dirty looks.

Pauline

4

A view from Craigwell

I live at Craigwell Avenue, Portadown along with my son. These past four years, we have suffered from the loyalists, who live roughly 300 yards away from me. I moved to Craigwell Avenue in November 1995. Since then the tension and trouble has got worse.

1996

During the trouble at Drumcree in 1996, the Orangemen were prevented from marching the Garvaghy Road. During the five days of the stand-off the tension was very high in our street. A heavy security presence moved in to Craigwell on 7th July. Around 10.00am on Thursday 11th July, the decision to ban the parade from the Garvaghy Road was reversed; at about 9.00pm, the loyalists' bonfire was lit. This bonfire – a yearly event – takes place about 800 yards from my house. Craigwell Avenue residents phoned the local police station roughly about five times from 8.00pm that evening to request security and protection at the top of Craigwell. Residents were told that the police were in the area, although the residents never saw any of them. My son was walking along the top of Craigwell around 8.30pm when he was hit on the head by a bottle thrown by someone in a red taxi. Again we phoned the police station and eventually they sent one landrover with two policemen inside. The policemen took a statement from my son and we pleaded with them to place a landrover at the top of Craigwell. They refused to do this, saying they were stretched to the limit due to trouble on the Garvaghy Road and the bonfire.

Later that evening a few stones were thrown at my house. They hit the window and broke the rain spout above the window. Again we phoned the local police station. They sent the same landrover that had been present a few hours before. Again they took a statement. The sat at the top of Craigwell for roughly one hour and then departed. Later on, at roughly one o'clock in the morning, one landrover returned and sat at the top of Craigwell. Around 1.50am we heard a lot of shouting and cheering. The next thing we knew, approximately fifty loyalists ran into Craigwell and the police landrover reversed halfway down the street. At this stage, I was standing at my bedroom window. I noticed that the loyalists were all masked and armed with baseball bats, sticks and Buckfast bottles. Suddenly my front door was kicked in. I grabbed my son and ran to the built-in wardrobe. The loyalist attackers completely wrecked my downstairs and ransacked the upstairs.

The wrecking in Craigwell took roughly five minutes. It wasn't until they left that we realized the full extent of the damage. As we walked outside, the street was like something from a war scene in a movie. When I looked around me, I couldn't believe what had actually happened. There were three ambulances there and the street was black with police. The police arrived just as around 200 loyalists were approaching the top of the street. The police fired plastic bullets to disperse the loyalist thugs. In the space of five minutes, the loyalists had managed, with a police presence, to wreck sixteen houses and completely demolish a car. All residents in the street were in a total state of shock. We couldn't believe that this had happened in the presence of a so-called loyal police force. Our street was in total disarray. There were women and children running everywhere.

The ambulance men and women checked all the residents and treated people in their homes. All the residents started the job of securing the houses. A local business man supplied wood and tools to board up houses. The police entered all of the houses to make sure it was safe for the residents to return to their homes and to survey the damage. As a result of what happened that night, the residents lost all remaining faith in the RUC. During the rest of that year there was the odd incident when stones were thrown at the houses and residents were cheered and jeered at.

1997

At the start of the next year, 1997, the tension grew worse. This was due to the murder of Robert Hamill. The residents were afraid to go up the town, so we avoided it as much as possible. For nights on end, loyalists at the top of Craigwell Avenue cheered and shouted about the murder of Robert Hamill. The Orangemen paraded the Garvaghy Road in 1997; but the residents of Craigwell Avenue still suffered. There was a heavy security presence in Craigwell the morning of the parade. Residents were very angry at the way Garvaghy Road residents were beaten and treated by the police. The heavy security presence remained in Craigwell after the parade and closed the top of the Craigwell Avenue off completely. Again, the 11th July bonfire was lit.

The next big event to affect the Craigwell Avenue residents was the murder of leading loyalist, Billy Wright. Loyalists once again took to the streets. A heavy security presence moved into Craigwell the afternoon of the shooting. The loyalists threw stones and shouted about Robert Hamill. Residents felt an awful unease that night, due to their lack of faith in the RUC to protect them. They kept watch over the street themselves in case the wrecking of houses took place again. Residents once again stayed out of the town and loyalists once again took over. Local businesses received phone calls from the Portadown branch of the LVF to close for Billy Wright's funeral or else! As if this wasn't bad enough, the Union Jack was lowered to half-mast in the town centre – as if he was a member of royalty! This event shocked residents, because this flag was not lowered for anyone else. It was as if Billy Wright was being thought of as a hero of some sort.

On Thursday 18th June, loyalists again entered Craigwell Avenue. Roughly around 10.50pm, iron bars were forced through the windows of my car, which was parked outside my house. The RUC were again present in Craigwell, although they were at the back of the houses dealing with another incident. One RUC man told my daughter he had seen the 'hooligans', although he couldn't do anything. Descriptions of the men were given to the police by neighbours who saw what they had done.

1998

Around 2.30am on 4th July 1998, security forces moved in to erect barricades at the top of Craigwell Avenue. When residents looked out their windows at this hour of the morning, they were greeted by the sight of army men and women blocking them in. Due to the amount of noise being made by army cranes and other machines, the residents were prevented from sleeping. When the children of Craigwell went outside the next morning they were really fascinated by what was happening around them. Residents had never seen such barricades at the top of the street before. Residents were more or less closed in. Portadown town centre was once again a no-go area. These barricades remained in Craigwell Avenue for a number of weeks because of illegal protests being held by loyalists at the top of Craigwell. Residents felt totally intimidated by these protests and continually asked themselves why loyalists were getting away with this.

The barricades remained in Craigwell Avenue until Sunday 19th July, and were removed without any consultation with the residents or local councillors. Residents once again felt a sense of unease. Two landrovers of police and two landrovers of army remained, but this did nothing to ease the residents' fear because the police were still on the frontlines. Residents' fears grew for what could happen now that the barricades were removed. As residents had guessed, when the barricades were removed, the illegal protests grew worse. We couldn't believe that this was being allowed to happen. On Friday 24th July, security forces allowed loyalists to once again enter Craigwell Avenue. To allow loyalists to do this, the RUC pushed and forced residents down the street using police dogs. Residents were appalled that they were once again pushed out of the way to accommodate loyalist hooligans.

At the moment, while I am writing this, the illegal protests are growing in size and happening more often. These protests are continuing in front of the police cameras, and a so-called neutral RUC.

Chrissie

5

Second-class citizens

Looking back, the siege of the nationalist part of Portadown started months before 6th July with everyone – nationalist and loyalist – waiting for the Parades Commission's verdict. Drumcree 1998 never left your mind, along with the Agreement and the Assembly elections. Would a 'Yes' vote help? Would we get the backing from the two governments? One minute you thought they can't let them march, the next minute you imagined they would let them march. For, in their terms, it would be the 'least worst' option.

But when the siege of Portadown started on the 6th July, it was to be a nightmare for two whole weeks! From the start of the march on Sunday morning, when the Orangemen marched by St. John's Church, what was to be a ten-minute walk lasted half an hour. Thousands upon thousands of Orangemen with their sashes and bowler hats and hundreds of hangers-on, cat calling and jeering and shouting 'Fenian bastards', 'McKenna's dogs', 'We will burn you all out in the middle of the night', jumping up and down, shouting 'Robert Hamill'. This was the Orange culture they where talking about. I left the church grounds when they had all passed, feeling nervous, fearful, wondering would the police and army stop them marching, or would Tony Blair cave in to them this year again.

As each day came and you watched the different spokepersons for the Orange Order, the fear grew by the hour. It was difficult to get a night's sleep. Even when you were tired, sleep wouldn't come. Nobody could relax. You could not walk from Obins

Street to the Garvaghy Road, because of the endless stream of Orangemen walking through Corcrain. When you got a lift in a car, the car was stopped and searched, even though the Orangemen were allowed free access to the Drumcree Church.

Every morning the loyalists gathered at the Tunnel Bridge. No one could get to their work. Talking to the police didn't help. All they would say was, 'There is nothing we can do'. Morning, noon, and night they marched, each day running into another. 'What day is it?' 'I don't know.' 'How many days has this been going on?' 'I can't remember', was the usual conversation. When the violence started at Drumcree Church, a new panic started. People watching television news bulletins saw the loyalists throwing blast bombs and petrol bombs, firing shots at the police and climbing over barricades. Women in their nightdresses, children in pyjamas, all terrified, were coming out of their houses looking for reassurance. You give it, but you need reassurance yourself. You still could not believe that the police would stand up to them. Everyone needs sleep but nobody could sleep.

When you are stuck behind the barricades you start to think the whole of the North is under siege, and if anything happens you are on your own. The siege mentality takes over. The world outside has forgotten about you. You no longer exist, and we are in a world of our own. You start to ask yourself questions. Why are the police and army there? Are they there to protect you or to keep you in your own part of town? We hear Harold Gracey, Davy Jones, Joel Patton and David McNarry calling for Orangemen to come in their thousands and help the Portadown brethren who are under siege; but they are not under siege. We are the ones under siege.

Then good news comes. Nationalist people from other areas are organising food and medical convoys to come to Portadown. At last we are not alone. One or two smaller convoys come to the Garvaghy Road. They get through without any trouble, but the larger one from Belfast is stopped on the Dungannon Road. Panic starts again. The bastards don't want people from outside to help us. After about an hour the police allowed the convoy to continue. The large crowd gathered at St. John's Chapel begins to clap and cheer when the first car enters through the barricades; we are not alone!

On Friday or Saturday morning, I am asked to go to Lurgan. When I arrive in Lurgan, I can not believe it; everything is normal. Men, women and children walking around, no talk of Drumcree, Garvaghy Road, or Orangemen. For the first time in over a week, I feel the tension draining out of me. I spend two hours, just walking about the streets of Lurgan. It was like a holiday, and when I returned to Portadown the gloom returned with me.

When I heard that three young brothers were burned to death in Ballymoney, I was filled with anger, hatred and guilt. Are they never going to stop? What is going to happen here on the 12th July? Why didn't we let them march? Is the death of the three Quinn brothers our fault? Why did we stop them? Why don't they go away and leave us alone? The Orange Order spokesperson gave an interview on television. The police had set up the innocent children, he claimed. It was everybody's fault. It had nothing to do with the Orange Order. Where was his feeling of guilt? Why do I feel guilty? I don't hate anybody, I didn't harm anybody! I didn't harm anybody! I didn't ask to be born into a ghetto! This march has nothing to do with the people on the Garvaghy Road. It is the Orange Order's fight against the Agreement and the Peace Process, the Orange card being played against the British government. All the violence and hatred I had seen all week didn't happen, I began to imagine. It was all in my mind!

When the Reverend Bingham made his statement at his church service and asked the Orangemen, in the light of what happened in Ballymoney, to pack up and go home, I got a small glimmer of hope. At last someone on the Orange side was getting some sense. On the 12th, when the expected crowd did not turn up, I at last began to think the protest was over, and when the police moved in to search the field and restrict the numbers going into it, I felt it was over. On television that night the police showed the guns and blast bombs found in the field. 'Surely,' I said, 'the Orange Order must accept once and for all it was finished.' But no! Davy Jones, the Orange Order spokesperson stated that the guns and bombs could have been planted by Republicans living in the nearby Ballyoran estate and asked for the brethren throughout the North to come to Portadown again! Thank God they didn't listen to him.

A couple of days later the barricades were removed from the Garvaghy Road. As far as the police and British government were concerned, the siege was over for another year. But this is not true. We, the nationalist people are under siege every day of the year, confined to a nationalist enclave, no amenities in our area, no cash point machines, no medical centre. All amenities, like the swimming pool, are in loyalist areas. There is no access to the town centre at night. Children are afraid to wear their school uniforms, because if someone recognises that they go to a Catholic school, they will be beaten up. No nationalist parades are allowed in the town centre. Nationalist bands are confined to nationalist areas. There are no rights for nationalists. Croppies lie down in Portadown! The siege of nationalist Portadown goes on!

The British government must address these wrongs. They must show the nationalist people they are not second class citizens. The police must act; they must not allow the Orange Order to rule again.

Labhras

6

They Just Don't Understand: Reflections on 1997

When I heard the '98 parade was to be banned from the road I thought it was just too good to be true. I remember watching Mo Mowlam coming and going from the Drumcree Centre in '97 and even though she seemed to be likeable person, I still couldn't bring myself to approach her. I'm not sure whether it was because of her importance or because of what they had done to us in '96. Anyway, I thought I'd wait a wee while and see what happened.

'97 started just like 1996. The Orangemen were saying the same things about us, the RUC had laid into our young lads after the Junior Orange parade in May, there were spotter planes and helicopters flying around every day, and now the army was setting up more barbed wire barricades to keep the Orangemen back from the police at Drumcree. Still, it wasn't until after Mo's visit on the Friday before the Sunday parade that I started to think maybe they really were going to keep their word this time.

I spent most of my time up at the women's Peace and Justice Camp or down at the Centre. The Camp was great craic, sitting out at night round the fire, watching the road and looking out at the lights of the town. People would go round and round in circles talking about what we thought was going to happen: 'They will – they won't' and 'They can – they can't'. Even when I was fed up with it I'd get stuck in again every time somebody started saying what they thought was going to happen. And when the ones that were beat off the road in '96 started talking about what happened to them, they would always turn it into a laugh and people would have tears in their eyes laughing. It's funny, it's like you were scared and laughing at the same time. I suppose we were just trying to laugh away our fear so that we could do it again.

There was only a handful of us at the camp when the siren went off the first time at 3 o'clock on Sunday morning. When we saw the Brits turning away down the Drumcree Road, we knew it was a false alarm and told the people that came running up the road shouting and screaming. I walked on home with some of them and I was just getting into bed when the siren went again. The helicopters were still up since the first alarm and my husband said it was probably just another false alarm, but you couldn't take that chance. I pulled my clothes on again and we ran for the road hoping to God we weren't going to be betrayed again. But even before we got out of the estate we could hear the plastic bullet guns and the shouting. I was so angry and afraid and disappointed, I nearly burst out crying, but I couldn't stop myself running for the road.

There were people running from every direction and trying to get past the police. They closed in on us from two sides with jeeps and revved the engines like they were going to drive over us. Then about a hundred of them came down the road firing plastic bullets into Ballyoran. They just marched right through a line of burning petrol somebody had spread to stop them and I thought they were going to wade right into us. They were beating their shields and shouting some peoples' names and to 'get so and so'! When they got near us, the jeeps switched their lights off and it was pitch dark. I thought they were going to kill us but then a camera crew shone their light on us and I think that's when the line of riot police stopped.

After a while somebody started saying the rosary. I wanted to scream at them to stop but I couldn't and I found myself getting onto my knees like most of the others. I could hear the Brits sniggering and I felt even worse about it. I wanted to run at them and tear the shields and helmets away from their faces.

They left us there for ages sitting on the road and I needed to go to the toilet, but I didn't want to leave the road in case I couldn't get back again. Some of the men went and pissed against the sides of jeeps and people laughed just at the idea of it. Then some of us took off our coats and made a screen beside a jeep where there was a road grating – so we could have some privacy. Still it was awful embarrassing and we shouted for people and cameramen not to be looking towards us; there was nothing else we could do.

It must have been about 4 o'clock when one of the news reporters said he had been told over the phone that it had just been announced that the Orangemen were to get their parade. That was when I remembered Mo Mowlam smiling at us and eating the Chinese take-away we gave her in the community centre. God, how I cursed her!

After a while the RUC told us we were breaking the law and we knew they were going to start on us like they did in '96. Everybody started to link arms and I took my glasses off. I can see nothing without them but I was afraid of getting glass in my eye. I could hear the police that were dragging people out calling them 'Fenian bastards' and all, and I could hear people roaring in pain when the cops kicked or stood on their legs or bent their wrists back. Sometimes you could hear people calling them 'Orange bastards' but sometimes you only heard a kind of a grunt because the cops had their arms around their throat or across their face when they dragging them away.

I was near the middle of the crowd and every time they stopped dragging people away, I put my glasses on again to see what was happening. There was a woman near me who I had fallen out with over something silly and we hadn't been speaking to each other for ages. When our eyes met all I could do was make one of them kind of smiles that says 'I'm sorry', and look away. I thought I might have looked away too soon or she might not have understood but she said hello the next time we met and I knew she did.

They must have stopped taking people away five or six times and every time they stopped, you would feel the tension drain out of you. We could hear the Welsh choir singing for a while but then the people outside the jeeps would start shouting and screaming and you'd get so scared just imagining what was happening and that it was going to get even worse when they started again. When people were being thrown out through the ring of cops and jeeps, there would be screaming and shouting and the camera crews would turn away from us. That's when this big brute of a cop would run in from the other side of the road and whack somebody with his baton, usually one of the fellas, and we would shout at the cameramen to keep looking at us. Some observers complained about him to the cops in charge but they said they couldn't identify him. There was a picture of him in the *Sunday Business Post* hitting a young fella sitting on the road.

Billy's wee fella was sitting near me and when it got a bit quieter, I could hear him kind of whimper or stifle little sobs. God help him, he was only about 12 years old. Some of us said to him that he should go but he wouldn't leave us. I don't know if it was because he was more scared to leave or because he was just so determined to stay on the road. Every time I think of him I feel so sad and so proud at the same time.

Some women were crying but the men tried not to show how scared they were; they always get the worst of it. Even though we were all scared, there was some laughing in the middle of it all. It must have been our nerves. There was a girl near me and all of a sudden she said, 'Jesus, I forgot to put my bra on'! – everybody laughed. All the women knew what she meant because we had talked about it at the Women's' Peace Camp. We knew the police would pull the clothes off us like they did the year before and we talked about what we would wear so that they couldn't do it again. I had about four layers of clothes on and a belt on my trousers. We didn't wear any jewellery or watches either because you would lose them or they'd get broken when they grab you or hit you.

A couple of people had mobile phones and they passed them round to anybody who wanted to phone their family and tell them they were alright and not to be worrying. Most of my family lives out in the country and they phoned my sister in Churchill Park to find out if I was alright. She was telling me

Left:
Unconscious
protestor
dragged
away by the
RUC

The RUC keeping Obins Street clear of nationalist protestors for the Orangemen's Drumcree parade, 1985. Below, the RUC watch over a group of protestors, including Joe Duffy (independent nationalist councillor) (also 1985). See page 135.

Bowler hats and balaclavas, July 1972. Having suppressed all opposition, the B
led loyalist paramilitaries into the Catholic 'Tunnel'/Obins Street area. As the picture
here they drilled and then formed a guard of honour for the Orangemen parad
Drumcree Church (see pages 13

Masked loyalist paramilitaries escort the Orangemen along the
Garvaghy Road on their return from Drumcree Church, July 1972

Drumcree 1996. The leaders of unionism and Orangeism approach the barricade at the bottom of Drumcree Hill. *From left to right:* David Trimble (MP), Geoffrey Donaldson (MP), the Rev. Martin Smyth (MP) and Harold Gracey (see page 152)

1995 — The residents say 'no' (see page 143)

Above: The Garvaghy Road Residents' Coalition, pictured with Rosemary Nelson

Photo: Mal McCann

A rally of residents 1997

Radio Equality in action (see pages 89-103)

The Women's peace and justice camp 1997, a few days
before it was overrun by units of the RUC and British army
'looking for weapons'

The 1997 invasion (see pages 163-166)

Invasion 1997

The residents are walled in by military fortifications and checkpoints (1998)

Loyalists controlling traffic outside the barrier at St John's (above)
while the RUC and British army look on (see pages 79-80)

Residents outside St John's church surrounded by makeshift British army/RUC barricade (1998)

RUC with plastic baton round weapons, lower Garvaghy Road (1997)

Three British Army helicopters (including two Chinooks) hover over the Garvaghy area, ferrying British troops to enforce the Parades Commission ruling, July 1998 (see page 168)

RUC chasing nationalist youths through the People's Park, February 1999,
following the arrival of a busload of Orangemen

Overseeing the siege of the Garvaghy Road, 1997

Resident of Craigwell Avenue holds up concrete block which loyalists put through her window in July 1996 (see pages 32-36)

Cardinal Daly hears firsthand accounts of loyalist attack on Craigwell Avenue, July 1996 (see pages 155)

The Garvaghy food convoy arrives from West Belfast, is held up and searched by the RUC… but finally gets through (1998). Meanwhile loyalists take weapons, including firearms, to Drumcree unhindered.

Above: Mural of Orangeman threatening Irish dancers with a petrol bomb, completed a few days before the petrol bombing and murder of the three Quinn brothers in Ballymoney, July 1998. *Below:* Quinn brothers' funeral

Above: Darren Murray, killed by a van while running away from loyalists who referred to him as the 'Fenian nigger' (see pages 85-88)

later that it was just about daybreak when they phoned and she could see me from her bedroom window in Churchill Park. She told them I was okay but she didn't tell them she was looking out at me sitting in the middle of the riot squad.

I was near the middle of the crowd and it was daylight when my turn came to be pulled away. I can't think what was in my head when they grabbed me only what I heard people shouting before ('You Orange bastards') and hoping they didn't rip my clothes away in front of the cameras. They dragged me through the two lines of jeeps and threw me out onto the Ashgrove Road. I didn't get it too bad but it was in between the jeeps that others got the worst beating. The cameras couldn't see what was being done to people in between the jeeps. When they threw me down, I got up and tried to run back in again. I don't know what was in my head; it was sort of automatic. Maybe I just couldn't accept what they were doing or that we were beaten again. It was only when I saw others do the same that I realised why people on the outside had been screaming and drawing the cameramen away from us. But if it wasn't for the people who were waiting to pick us up and hold us back, we would have been battered senseless. I could see by the wrinkles at the corner of their eyes that they (the RUC) were smiling behind their masks and visors. They were delighted with themselves and were mocking and taunting us.

It was only when it was all over that I let myself cry. I was physically and mentally exhausted.

That was 1997 and now it's just a month to July 1998 and we might have to go through it all again. I suppose people will say we don't have to go through it if we don't want to, that we could draw our blinds or go away. You just have to live in Portadown to understand why we do it. Most of my family lives outside the town and I can hardly explain it to them. They worry about me and my husband and they say we should take a holiday away from the road this year. 'What difference will one or two people make', they say. I say it's like the pain of having a baby' its something you have to go through and you don't really want to go through it – but at the same time you want to go through with it. But I think they just don't understand.
Ann

7

The town I would love to say 'I love so well!'

Coping with four young children, one of whom is just approaching her first birthday, which falls in the school summer break, is not easy. My second youngest also celebrates her birthday in the school summer break, 12th July, a public holiday. She was six, July past. When she turned one, we had a birthday party and we all had a good time, but then we were all on holiday. That was the last party she had.

For the past five years we have spent July in Portadown, which is very unfortunate, because we live on the Garvaghy Road. I am a single parent and being out of work (from September 1983) I cannot afford a holiday. There is so much stress, pressure and uncertainty. To have a birthday party is out of the question. We are afraid to relax for a few hours, for fear that outside my front door becomes a battle zone. I have lived in the North of Ireland for 32 years. I am very aware of the tension, the hatred, the fear and the division between the two communities.

My three older children have attended an integrated school for the past four years. I have never witnessed anything like the tension, hatred and fear that has ripped through Portadown (I can only speak for Portadown). This has been very worrying and terrifying, for not only have I witnessed this, but my children have also witnessed it, too. I am finding it very hard to cope. Will they ever understand what has happened?

In September, my eldest son will be starting secondary education and he will not be attending an integrated school. I am frightened to send him to an integrated school. For him to have an integrated education would mean leaving the community. He does not want to go, because he is afraid to be recognised as not only a Catholic, but a Catholic from the Garvaghy Road. He will not go shopping with me. I have been verbally abused because I am a Catholic from the Garvaghy Road.

When I go shopping, I suffer from panic attacks. We cannot go to the local swimming pool on a family outing. The children have so much energy; the swimming pool is a good way to release it. It is very painful to watch my children as Drumcree has had traumatic effects on their behaviour. The questions they ask are very hard to answer. They do not understand why the police and army have set up checkpoints. 'Why do helicopters fly in the sky above us? Why are our Protestant neighbours protesting?' I have no answer for them. They also ask, 'Was Portadown like this when you were a wee girl, mummy?' 'It was', I always answer.

The thousands might have left Drumcree. The siege, to the outside world, may seem over, but not for us. We are living mentally under siege! Every night, when my children are sleeping safe and sound in their beds, I have one of my quiet moments. I question myself, do I really want to bring my children up in a town infested with hatred and fear, where they will have a sense of nothingness, or do I stay and struggle to be recognised as we are, and hope and pray? The reason why I question myself on staying or leaving is because, when I went out of town to visit friends, I enjoyed my few hours away from Portadown. I wasn't tense; I wasn't afraid. My children were playing freely and were doing as children do. They were enjoying themselves; they were having fun. As we were leaving, the mood changed; they were tense and so was I. It was then I realised we are not living a normal life.

Why is this happening to us? I don't want my children to grow up resenting the Protestant community. I fear they will get sucked into the tit-for-tat violence. I do not want to suppress their identity, but I want them to survive. We need to be relieved of this pressure we are living under.

To cope, I am going to go on tranquilisers.

Claire

Protestant fundamentalist leaflet (1998) depicting British Prime Minister Tony Blair in the ruins of a burnt out Catholic Church, with quotes apparently providing biblical justifications for such actions.

8

A Catholic in Portadown

I have spent all my life in my home town of Portadown. As a child, my life was restricted by the Orange Order. As a teenager, I witnessed verbal abuse in my work place because of the Orange Order parades. My father's theory was, 'Keep your head down and your mouth shut, if you want to survive.' 'It will all be over in a couple of days,' was one of his sayings.

Well, 56 years have passed and it is not all over! These peaceful protests about Orange parades did not start in 1995. This community has always objected to and never ever wanted Orange parades through their area. I remember peaceful protests, tea parties from the 1980s.

I never took a sedative in my life until this year. I witnessed the events of 1997 and I am very fearful of an Orange attack on the nationalist community. A Protestant friend once told me, 'Pray that the Orange Order never attack this area. They would gladly leave every one of you dead!' This was said 15 years ago.

I suffer headaches and nervous tension. I'm smoking even more and I have developed a rash on my face – caused by stress. I fully support my community and the Coalition. Thank God for great speakers and determined people! I am also determined. Having no family of my own, I adore my young nephew and niece that live in the Ballyoran estate. This problem must be solved. There is no way I will have any RUC beating them off the road in ten years' time.

For many years I have rarely gone shopping in the town centre. I shop via a catalogue for clothes, and everything else I can get along the Garvaghy Road. Now, I refuse to allow my younger sister and her young family to travel alone into the town centre, in case she is met with physical or verbal abuse.

My whole life has been restricted by the Orange Order. I'm getting to the point where I would gladly move to Dundalk or Sligo, in order to have some form of normal life – if only my family would move too.

Perhaps I should seek political asylum from the government fund? After all, it is dangerous to be a Catholic in Portadown!

Marie

9

My diary of Drumcree

Wednesday 17th June

Attended a meeting in St. Mary's Hall; the hall was packed. This was a very different meeting tonight. Before, I felt that the community looked to Breandán Mac Cionnaith and the Coalition for guidance and advice. Now the community were laying down the rules! Their nerves are on edge. This community is determined that the Orange Order is not walking through their area. They were so uptight that many couldn't take in a lot Breandán was saying and some were downright rude to him! Breandán has great patience and he fully understands this community's feelings. The call was strong for thousands of people to come to the Garvaghy Road to support us this year.

Tuesday 18th June

Papers are full of the 'Tour of the North' parade in Belfast. It has been re-routed! Will this event pass off peacefully? Garvaghy Road quiet, but anxious.

Saturday 20th June

Large parade in Portadown town centre tonight. Pouring rain – perhaps this will help to keep numbers down and the town quiet.

Sunday 21st June

'Ban Drumcree and we'll close Ulster'; papers full of Drumcree.
Reports of a loyalist backlash closing the ports and ferries.
Loyalists have threatened to bring Northern Ireland to a
standstill. There have been rumours that the parade is banned
from going down the road. Flanagan, head of the RUC,
apparently has told a journalist in Belfast in April that if loyalists
gather in their thousands he'll let the parade through! Everyone
is very anxious and frightened!

I'm like an old mother hen. I want my son and daughter (who
is expecting her third child on 4th July) and my grand-daughter
with me to keep them safe – this is laughable, for if the parade
is going down the road, I intend to peacefully protest with the
rest of my community. I'm constantly on the phone, telling my
son who lives and works in Belfast to take care and my daughter
who lives in Lurgan to do the same.

Monday 22nd June

Nationalist community 'panicking'. People talking about buying
in extra food, candles, etc. How are the ones on the dole going
to manage this; it will be hard for them. I've never seen so
many people smoking cigarettes in all my life! Many women
that I have spoken to have contacted their doctors for sedatives.
Apparently there is no bother getting any sedative you fancy.
My own sister who never took a tablet in her life has got a
prescription for Roche 5s. Once she gave the doctor her address
– Garvaghy Road – these drugs were dished out like sweets!
Many mothers are laying in Calpol to help the children sleep
through any trouble!

Everyone is expecting a slaughtering match from the RUC.
People are saying that it will be only after nationalist coffins
are carried up the Garvaghy Road that the problem will be
solved.

This is an awful way to live. The tension and stress on the
whole community is obvious. Perhaps I notice it more as I'm
living back in Portadown after an absence of twenty-three years.
Yet I only lived a few miles down the road – in Brownlow.

There are no parades in Brownlow. A few kerbs painted red, white and blue or green, white and orange. Each estate has different wall murals – but no Orange parades. So I feel quite angry at the Orange Order demanding to parade through this area; they could be allowed yet again, when this community doesn't want this and all we are asking for is equality and to live in peace.

Tuesday 23rd June

Trimble seems adamant that the Orange Order will walk the Garvaghy Road. He has called on Gerry Adams, Sinn Féin, to call his dogs off. Dear God, now we're 'dogs!' Can no one within the Protestant family sit down – go back to the drawing board and look at why these troubles started? Surely they can't all believe that the nationalist people in the 60's were fed up not working and producing large families and just wanted to start a war! There never was equality for nationalists in Northern Ireland and the Protestant hate for Catholic people is responsible for this inequality. At this I get very frustrated and angry that no one seems to listen to the nationalists.

Wednesday 24th June

Media full of election promises. Still undecided – vote 'Yes' or 'No'? In the end, I place my trust in Sinn Féin. After all, Bobby Sands, hunger-striker, was a politician!

Thursday 25th June

Voting Day. Everyone anxious about the result.

Friday 26th June

Election results coming in. Sinn Féin holding well. A dear and best friend, Sheena Campbell, RIP, (shot dead by UFF in Belfast) would be proud!

Sunday 28th June

Tunnel Fleadh. Everything went well. This event helped to lift people's spirits as the whole community is anxious as to what will happen next Sunday. This community is one unit – everyone is suffering as one.

Monday 29th June

The Parades Commission has re-routed the Orange Order from walking the Garvaghy Road! At last, I feel for the first time in 47 years that I am a citizen of my own town. For once, the nationalists have the law on their side and it feels good! The Orange Order is predicting widespread violence. Was interviewed by Channel Four with Clare Dignam and asked how I felt about the Orange Order's threat. I said it was a sad day for me because by law the Orange Order were being forced to accept me as an equal, a citizen of Portadown, Northern Ireland. If they had voluntarily re-routed, there would have been a better chance of true cross-community work and a great future for Portadown and Northern Ireland. Let's face it – if the problem can be solved in Portadown, it can be solved throughout Northern Ireland. I believe the problem is only simmering. Their hatred for nationalists will go even deeper, if they don't talk to the Coalition and compromise – reach a decision.

Everyone is waiting with bated breath! Will there be another siege? Will the Labour government give into their demands?

Tuesday 30th June

Media starting to arrive. The Orange Order is adamant they will walk the road. Residents apprehensive about the British government backing down.

Wednesday 1st July

Everyone 'buying-in' in case there is another siege. Hell! Of course there will be another siege! All the residents know this. They talk of nothing else. Friends, family, and neighbours have only one thing on their minds – will the nationalists be beaten off the road again?

Thursday 2nd July

Reporters interviewing local people and members of the Garvaghy Road Women Writers' Group. Women's Camp is

set up tonight. Unable to attend as my six year old grand-
daughter is staying with me. Her mum has safely delivered a
beautiful baby boy. Thank God, she'll be home by Sunday!

Friday 3rd July

I helped to see the Obins Street kids safely off to Dublin on
holiday. Visited the hospital. Joined the Women's Camp until
3.00am. Great meeting in St. Mary's Hall tonight. This
community is like one large family. Everyone very proud of
Breandán Mac Cionnaith, Joe Duffy and all the Coalition. Large
convoy of army passed the Women's Camp at 3.00am. This
frightened the women. The army, though, had phoned through
to Joe Duffy, for him to warn the women that it was loading for
Drumcree.

Saturday 4th July

Joined the Women's Peace Camp at 10.30am. Bright sunny
day, women laughing and smoking – but it's a nervous laugh.
Everyone remembering back to 1997. We are all still very fearful
that the British government will cave in and force down the
parade.

Women's Camp closed at 3.00pm. Community Vigil at
6.00pm. Large turn out for this. The media are everywhere!
Proximity talks taking place between the Residents' Coalition
and the Orange Order. Meeting in Community Centre 11.00pm.
People out walking about – can't settle until they hear the
outcome of this meeting. Spread news – the parade is not going
through!

Sunday 5th July

Garvaghy Road very quiet. Few tents erected. Large security
presence and media. Orange Order walks past roundabout at
St. John's Chapel. A small gathering of nationalists stand quietly
and observe. Large presence of Orangemen! Some shout abuse
and jump up and down, shouting out Robert Hamill's name.
Watch the parade gather at Drumcree on TV. Whole community
tuned into our local community radio, Radio Equality. Local

bulletins given constantly. This station has become a life-line for the community, keeping them in touch with the situation. By 4.00pm, hundreds of cars, bumper to bumper, make their way to Drumcree. It has been reported that there are between 4,000-5,000 Orangemen gathered. Why are so many allowed?

Rioting has broken out in Belfast and Derry in loyalist areas. Helicopters hover overhead. 12.00pm, Garvaghy Road quiet. Stewards can be seen walking about. Many of the community slowly walking about speaking in hushed tones, everyone very fearful – please God don't let the RUC and army turn on us!

Monday 6th July

Town centre open but quiet. Roads to airports and ferries operating as normal. Local radio station a great comfort and help. Mo [Mowlam] adamant that the Orange Order is not walking the Garvaghy Road. Paisley visited Drumcree last night.

Tuesday 7th July

News of thugs stopping people getting to work. Atmosphere very tense along the Garvaghy Road. I'm helping out with the local radio station. Glad of something to do. Crowds gathering in the Drumcree field. Heavy security presence everywhere. Crowds storm the barricades in the field – RUC fire plastic bullets. Nationalists very anxious – suggest to Sister Laura that perhaps we could get a prayer meeting or rosary organised – something for the people to do. Interviewed by UTV describing situation here.

Wednesday 8th July

Worked with the Community Radio. There are many observers and visitors here. The Community Centre is a hive of activity.

Thursday 9th July

Orange Order visits Tony Blair in London. He remains firm on the Parades Commission decision. Large convoy of food arrives from West Belfast. Convoy is attacked before entering the

Garvaghy Road. My brother phoned to say that he received a
phone call from a woman, threatening me and all my family.
Recognised me from my interview on TV.

Friday 10th July

Atmosphere very, very tense. No one getting much sleep from
the noise from the field and helicopters hovering above. Parades
to the field begin each evening at 7.00pm. All hell breaks loose
about 10.30pm. Thank God I don't have any young babies to
worry about!

Sunday 12th July

Stand-off now one week old. Crowds continue to gather, shout
abuse, riot with the RUC and army, even though three young
brothers [the Quinn children] died in a fire caused by a petrol
bomb thrown by a loyalist. Roars from the field can be heard
clearly along with nail bombs, plastic bullets, etc. This has
become a nightly event. It is impossible for anyone in the
nationalist area to get a good night's sleep!

Monday 13th July

Orange parade held in Lurgan today. Because of the three boys'
deaths, numbers are down out at the field. From 11.00pm,
fireworks could be heard. Stood in the field with many of the
community and listened to them. Many nationalists argue that
the 'security forces' are handling the Orange Order with 'kid
gloves'. 'If that was us, we'd be dead by now,' remarked one
pensioner. 'About time they stood up to them,' remarks another.
Standing in that field was like watching an outdoor movie!
Paisley visited them again. He could be heard clearly inciting
them to walk the Garvaghy Road. Shots are fired – gunfire –
nail bombs, fireworks, plastic bullets; helicopters are up until
5.00am.

Tuesday 14th July

Things are very, very quiet, so quiet it's frightening. No one
in the nationalist area is sleeping well or eating normally. Many
are complaining of stomach pains, headaches, being very

nervous and scared. Play activities have been arranged for the children to give them as normal holiday as possible. The nightly prayer meetings were welcomed and well attended. Many people returning from holidays to find the problem not solved!

6th August 1998

The Orange Order has not walked the Garvaghy Road yet! Every night there have been attempts to 'take the road'. Security has been scaled down. The media have left. These illegal parades are allowed to gather. The result is intimidation and violence nightly, yet no one is arrested. The nationalist community is still under siege.

There are reports of verbal abuse in supermarkets and the 'tension' can be felt in the town centre. Many friends are traveling to Lurgan to shop. Friends who visit me from Lurgan have to travel home via the Moy and Dungannon Roads because of the illegal gatherings. The media are not reporting these nightly events – giving the impression that the Portadown problem has been solved.

My grand-daughter has not been to visit from July. Her mother is fearful of her being in Portadown when trouble breaks out. When I visit them in Lurgan, I must phone home to check where the illegal parade is being held, so I don't drive into any trouble. Friends and family always phone to ask where they should avoid. It is not always possible to tell them. Sometimes I don't hear about events until the next day. My whole life seems to revolve around these Orange thugs! I am a law-abiding citizen of Northern Ireland. I had a British passport – where are my rights?

Everyone is fearful of the dark nights settling in. The RUC are not trusted. Many believe they will turn a blind eye and allow them to walk. Already, many nationalists are talking about next year. The 1999 countdown has begun! At least the festival on the 14th and 15th August is stirring some excitement in the young again. The Orange Order are requesting that the Parades Commission allow them to walk the road on 15th August.

I am uneasy about next week's festival. The Orangemen's request will probably be turned down again leaving them very, very angry. They will know that we have a festival planned. They will probably see our festival as 'triumphalism', celebrating their defeat, and I believe they will attempt to take the road by gathering at every entrance to the Garvaghy Road. The 'slaughtering match' could well be on 15th August! (God forbid).

The hatred for Catholics in this town is pure evil. On Friday 7th August at 5.30pm many young Protestants, no more than twelve years of age, were taunting the RUC and army at Charles Street. Many women joined them later. How can there be any hope for true cross-community work in this town? I feel that nationalists are somehow going to have to compromise yet again, in order to bring things back to some show of normal life.

How has all this strain and stress affected me personally? Well, a headache for me was a rare complaint, now I suffer them daily. I feel drained mentally, physically and emotionally. I'm angry and frustrated that no one is listening or seems to care about the nationalists along the Garvaghy Road and surrounding area. I have a real fear that the problem is only 'simmering'. I feel restricted – under siege, and this makes me angry! I now am asking myself – do I want to live in Portadown? Life is too short for all this stress and strain and yet I'm also asking myself – why should I move away? I was born and reared in Portadown. It's my town too. I have a right and I demand the right to be accepted as a citizen of my town and country! It is a shame and disgrace that this community is suffering at the hands of Unionism and the Orange Order.

Unionists must recognise that events have moved on socially and economically as well as politically. The tragedy is that the philosophy of unionism has not evolved. Unionists must accept that a philosophy comprehensible in the 1920s is no longer acceptable in 1998.

I am proud of and I respect the nationalist community of Portadown for their behaviour and tolerance throughout this very stressful time.

Phil

10

A Steward's View

How do you begin to put down on paper your feelings concerning the events of Drumcree 1998, especially if you are a life-long resident of the Garvaghy Road area?

For me it began on Friday night, 3rd July. I had decided to spend that night at the Women's Peace and Justice Camp on the hill at Ballyoran. In the early hours, a convoy of lights and the roar of heavy engines filled the air. This was a convoy which stretched the entire length of the Garvaghy Road and it was made up of trucks, Saracens and lorries laden with diggers, barbed wire, floodlights and generators.

Surprisingly, no one in the encampment panicked, but we were all apprehensive. This was either for our protection or to keep us well hemmed into our own area. Within hours, a ring of steel was erected at every road leading into our community. The fourth Drumcree siege had begun. Leading up to Drumcree, we had been referred to as caged animals of various descriptions – in numerous news bulletins – by a senior politician. We are no animals, but we were certainly caged in. Events from here on in took place at a hectic pace. International observers arrived and supporters from all over Ireland flooded the area and were housed with local families, who were only too willing to show their hospitality in any way they could.

To try and account for what happened on a day-to-day basis is virtually impossible as one day ran into another so quickly and unnoticed by everyone.

I was given the task of organising the stewards throughout the area at potential hot spots such as St. John's Church, Ballyoran, Churchill, Garvaghy, the Tunnel and Park Road. A meeting was called in the Drumcree Centre at 7.00pm every night; and every night, as time went on, the number of men, women and young people increased. We knew the seriousness of the situation and responded accordingly. A total alcohol ban was imposed throughout the area and adhered to by everyone, especially the young people, whom I must say, acted with great restraint and dignity throughout the whole ordeal.

Armbands were distributed, as were walkie-talkies, and instructions were given. Our all-night vigilance had begun. We didn't know when it would end, but we were prepared for a long haul. A debt of gratitude must be given to these stewards who endured long hours and extremely bad weather, who not only maintained a presence in the area, but also maintained a presence in their places of employment as well.

By Tuesday, a convoy of food had arrived thanks to the people of Lurgan, and was received amidst tears and cries of joy. Surely the rivalry between Portadown and Lurgan people ended at that very moment! A day or two later, another convoy of cars and vans arrived from the people of Belfast. Never have I seen such amounts of food and witnessed such support from people who truly identified with our situation. Because of this generosity every household in our area was given food parcels, with our main priorities being old age pensioners and single parents.

Thursday night brought some 20,000 Orangemen to Drumcree Church with the threat of 100,000 descending on 12th July. Between the noise of fireworks, blast bombs, gunfire and bands playing the same two tunes, 'God Save the Queen' and 'The Sash', sleep for us was virtually impossible.

I went into work on the Tuesday and found myself hemmed in again as two blast bombs were left at the factory gates. Wednesday brought with it the worry that my only sister had been brought to Craigavon Hospital to have her baby. It was impossible to leave the area to try and get over to her and my brother-in-law, as we couldn't be guaranteed safe passage to and from the hospital. Thousands of loyalists gathered daily in the town centre and at strategic points, making safe access in and out of the area virtually impossible. By 3.30pm she had given birth to a baby girl and within 24 hours she was home; another crisis overcome.

The Drumcree Centre was kept open 24 hours a day, thanks to the hard work of the members of the co-operative. Sandwiches, casseroles, stews and pots of soup arrived in a steady stream from people to feed our visitors. These were greatly appreciated. Kitchen duties were taken on by everyone, on a two-hour rota system.

The 12th July didn't bring 100,000 Orangemen, but the death of three brothers, Jason, Mark and Richard Quinn, burned alive in their Ballymoney home. Words cannot express heartbreak, and this occasion was no exception. Every face I looked at around me, expressed the same feeling, 'That could so easily have been my kids, nephews or grandchildren.' I expected a flood of people to apply pressure on this community to allow Orange feet on the Garvaghy Road following this tragedy, but not one, to my recollection, uttered the words. This will never ever be looked upon as a victory to the people of the Garvaghy Road, but the sheer waste of young, innocent, human lives, which broke all our hearts.

Proximity talks were hastily arranged in Armagh, but I held no confidence in them. Not because I knew the Coalition couldn't broker a deal – they have always been open to discussion – but past experience had taught us that the Orange Order had a one-track mind: feet on the Garvaghy Road at any cost, even at the expense of the lives of three innocent children.

This saga will go on, for how long no one can predict. Weeks later, the Orangemen's protest still takes place at Drumcree, as does our own ever-increasing vigilance. The one thought that I will always carry with me of Drumcree '98 is that never before have I seen this community so united, resourceful and at one with each other. Can we go through another Drumcree? Do we want to? Will it be at the cost of more lives? I don't even want to contemplate answering these questions now, but as sure as there are clouds in the sky, the first Sunday in July will come again in 1999 and these and other questions must and will be answered.

Lastly, an enormous debt of gratitude must be paid to every member of the Garvaghy Road Coalition. The world must realise that they are nothing more than ordinary, everyday people who want nothing only fair play, equality and peace to live within this area. And most importantly, this community is consulted on every issue and aspect of Drumcree, and no decisions are taken by them without the full consent of the people.

Rose

11

A Child of the Garvaghy Road

July always comes too early for me. I just wish everything could get sorted out. I think it is appalling and very upsetting to see my friends and family being beaten on television by the RUC. At night I would lie in bed thinking of all the terrible things that could happen when the siren goes off. I would imagine it in my head, people fighting and being beaten off the Garvaghy Road. My mum doesn't smoke, but she gets so nervous she starts. On the first night I thought it was exciting and new, but soon I realized that it wasn't. I lay in bed one night thinking of all the things that could happen to me. The RUC is on the Orangemen's side and will probably help them do anything.

It was the first Sunday, and my mum had to 'man the phones', so I stayed the night in the club. I was really excited and my mum couldn't get me asleep, so she asked Rosie to take me for a walk. Rosie, Donna, Karen and her friend took me for a long walk around the park. Rosie's husband was meant to be standing guard at the bottom of Ballyoran, but when we got there, nobody was there. Rosie got all annoyed and then suddenly 'Boo', out of the blue, he jumped up behind a wall and scared us all. We stopped to talk to him for a while, and then saw seven or eight cars going up the hill towards the chapel. We started walking towards the chapel; every step I took I got even more nervous. Everywhere was filled with police and army. Rosie rushed me back to the club and I helped keep photographers and reporters out.

The next day at about 3.00pm, I went home. I lay on the sofa with a pillow and blanket, watched TV and soon fell asleep. At about 7.00pm I went back to the Centre. I started getting bored so I helped in the kitchen. Helping out in the kitchen was fun because I got to make tea for people and give out juice and biscuits to the children.

The whole community helped to make a buffet for foreigners and people from the Centre who helped out. I helped set out the buffet and butter bread. People soon came eating the food and then replacing it with empty trays.

If some one had asked me at that very moment if I thought the Orangemen would get down the road, I would have said 'yes', because I don't have one bit of confidence in the RUC or the British army.

When the food from Belfast came, I felt really good because that made me feel that people were thinking of us. The whole community helped sort out the food, even the children. I felt confident then that the Orangemen wouldn't get down the Road.

When I was a child of seven or eight, I was awakened to a terrible reality about life in Portadown. My father is very smart and could have been anything he wanted; he helped me write this letter. But he is a Catholic and was refused jobs because he is a Catholic. Now he is a labourer and that is all he knows how to be, so that's what he will stay.

I am only 11 years old and have already been chased and verbally abused out of the town centre (how many 11 year old Protestant girls could say the same?). If maybe the Orangemen were more sensitive and caring they would have more respect and choose a different road for their march.

It is now 25 November 1998; the Orangemen did not get down the Road. They are still holding a protest every Saturday and evenings. We the Catholics of Portadown are still being chased out of the town and are very upset about this (some things never change). I now have a little trust in the RUC, but I would not hold my breath for the Orangemen not getting down the Road next year.

Meg

12

'There's Orangemen, Daddy'

I am sitting here in my living room in the middle of April thinking it won't be long to Drumcree again. My wife starts panicking. She says, 'Oh no! Not Drumcree again!'. Her nerves start to go and she starts worrying and thinking about the house, and how they parade by at two o'clock in the morning, banging their drums and shouting.

My young boy says, 'Remember Drumcree I, dad, when they threw stones at our house and bottles and the police told you to put us in the car and make us lie down on the floor and get out as fast as we could?'

My wife's nerves start to go about May and her stomach hurts right until Drumcree is over. I have to listen to her saying, 'July is coming, July is coming', every day from May. Every July, at some stage, we have to leave our home and live with my wife's mother and sister. The children and my wife and I have to lie on the floor of one of these houses; it is an awful way to live but what can we do?

I never forget one night during Drumcree last year (1998), the street was in darkness as the lights were out and around 2am in the morning the Orangemen and their bands came parading down and they stopped at the entrance to our street playing 'Derry's Walls', and shouting abuse. My younger daughter took an asthma attack. She could not breathe. I had to go and get the inhaler and put her on it. She was nearly blue and my wife thought she was going to die on us.

My wife and I think we came through hell over Drumcree and we are thinking of selling our house. The only problem is that Drumcree has hurt us again, as it has knocked down the value. Estate agents now call it a non-desireable area.

This year has been the worst, as from 5th July the Orangemen have paraded every night of the week. They have thrown fireworks and my three year old child cannot sleep. Every time she hears a bang, she says, 'There's the Orangemen back, daddy'. I brought her up the town one Saturday and came out of Wellworths, and there, Orangemen were protesting. They started to fight and she was afraid and started to cry.

Last Saturday I went to town, so I took her up with me. She saw the police landrovers and started to cry and would not go up. She shouted, 'There's Orangemen, there's Orangemen, daddy, there's Orangemen!'

I just wish Mr David Jones could see what he and his Orangemen are doing to my family. Mr McNarry has said that Mr Mac Cionnaith has created a monster on the Garvaghy Road. Well, I think Mr McNarry has created the monster, and it's that big and violent, he can't get it killed.

Would Mr Jones like to have to leave his home? Are his children afraid to live in their own home and live in fear of July every year, all because Orangemen want to step over their Catholic neighbours?

Just the other Saturday night, the bands, the shouting, and the fireworks were going off until 3am in the morning, and the children were up most of the night. My wife sat up and would not go to bed, afraid of them attacking our house.

This is an awful way to live your life, all because the LOL can't get down one road. With all the roads they can walk, why does the RUC not move them away from the one area where they are not wanted?

The past four years have been a disaster for me and my family, having to move every year, all because the LOL want to walk a road were they are definitely not wanted. My family are refugees every July, living in my sister-in-law's or my mother-in-law's. Apart from the fear, the worst about being a refugee are the little things – not sleeping, not knowing where things are kept, worried the kids will damage the furniture, and outstaying hospitality.

I just wish the Drumcree trouble was over and the Orange Order would see sense and sit down and talk to their Catholic neighbours and work out something, so we could all enjoy our summer in peace and my family could live in our house without being afraid. I can just live in hope that one day it will happen.

Martin

13

A Corcrain Mother's Thoughts

I am a working mother of a grown-up family, living at home. I live in a small nationalist cul-de-sac, off the main Corcrain Road, which runs parallel to the Garvaghy Road. This area is on the fringe of the nationalist area of Portadown and because of its proximity to a loyalist area, is considered a 'flash-point'.

In previous years, the unrest caused by Drumcree was limited because the Orange parade was pushed through the road regardless. This year, however, is very different because for the first time the Orange Order have had their so-called church parade curtailed by a legal body, namely the Parades Commission. The resulting harassment of the nationalists has been a frightening and intimidating experience. As for my family and myself, I can only say that even as a relatively strong person with good nerves, I have found the whole episode, this year, very awesome and sinister.

Most of my neighbours have young children and left to holiday over the Drumcree period – this left my family feeling vulnerable and isolated, considering our house is just a field away from a loyalist stronghold. At night, groups gathered near, and in this field, to ritualistically beat drums and shout sectarian abuse. It was especially frightening when the street lights had mysteriously been extinguished and most of the cul-de-sac was in pitch blackness, except for the helicopters overhead with searchlights and their almost constant penetrating sound.

Even simple things like crossing the road to the shop or taking the dog for a walk were grossly unpleasant, because of the constant presence of groups of individuals going to and coming from the 'field' at Drumcree. These individuals, dressed in red, white and blue regalia (generally), did everything they could to make you feel threatened, without actually touching you – such as walking four to five abreast to force you to leave the pavement, staring directly into your face, then sniggering.

On one evening, when my eldest son was returning home, a person coming from Drumcree 'field' walked alongside him – a total stranger – and taunted him. When my son ignored him and walked faster, he started to also walk faster and push up against him, saying, 'I know what you are and where you are going.' On another night I had just returned from the shop across the road. I brought out a watering can to water plants and I observed a figure walking towards my house. In the dusk I thought it was my neighbour, but he passed and proceeded to go over the fence into the field which leads to the Corcrain Estate. As he got to the other side of the fence he stopped, looked over at me and shouted, 'See you; if you snitch on me, I'll be back to get you!' I had not a clue what he was talking about, but he alarmed me so much that I telephoned the RUC station. My husband, who was in the front bedroom, heard him clearly and came down, but there was no sign of him. We discovered the next day that the person was probably responsible for threatening the female owner of the shop and breaking her car window, as she drove off from her premises. The police telephoned me the next day to say they thought he threatened me because he had seen me coming from the shop minutes before he jumped out at the owner, and thought I had seen him.

In August, on two evenings when loyalist mobs gathered at Shillingtons, my mother, aged 72 years, who has had three cardiac operations over the years, had to do a six mile detour in her car before she could safely call to my home. This mob was allowed to gather only a few yards from a police patrol. This was the last straw and I telephoned Knock Road Police Station and complained to Assistant Chief Constable Craig. He was courteous, but did say that they wanted things to remain 'low-key'! One wonders how 'low-key' things would be viewed by the RUC if a nationalist mob dared to impede traffic!

One felt safer up at the Drumcree Centre. A sense of camaraderie prevailed there, but then there was the problem of walking back to the house. One night I was escorted to my house by five security force personnel, and this well before midnight! It is now 10th August and still the local lodge of the Orange Order are talking about marching down the Garvaghy Road. It is sad when grown men regress back to toddlers and cannot accept the word, 'no'.

Moya

Loyalist hymn of hate, referring to the 1996 siege and Trimble's meeting with Billy Wright

GET YOURSELF A SASH

It was on the 7th of July in the year of '96
Our loyal brethren found themselves in a fix.
The Garvaghy march halted on the order of Sir Hugh,
So they were stuck in Drumcree wondering what to do.
Well, they commandeered a digger,
And the army got one bigger!
While Sir Patrick tried to figure,
A way to get them through.

Day after day, yea and night after night,
Trimble jigged over headstones spoiling for a fight.
Tempers were a-flaring, the mood was getting tense,
So in came the Para's with a great big ten foot fence.
Brave Davy wasn't daunted by this hurdle built so tall,
He just sent for the U.V.F who rallied to his call.
While the Para's with their spot-lights put up a concrete wall!

Big Ian marched in amid all the ballyhoo.
Storming to the front lines, to see what he could do.
He puffed, he blew, he did rant and roar,
Yet he didn't do any fighting in 1944
He should remember to practice what he preaches
Where were his loyalties on far-off Normandy Beaches
For all our present troubles, he must surely share the blame
As for being titled Reverend he should hang his head in shame.

On the eve of the "Twelfth" the order it went out,
Get the loyal 'Orangies' down their favourite route.
Force all the Fenian b-------s from the Queens Highway,
Beat the women senseless, keep those peasants all at bay.
This they did with truncheons heavy, and baton rounds galore
They were willing and ruthless, cos they'd done it all before.

Meanwhile Mayhem supported our Sir Hugh,
Who said "to avoid violence" what else was he to do???
And so between the both of them
THE ORANGEMEN GOT THROUGH.
There is a little lesson here, learn it in a flash
Get yourself a SASH.

14

Fourteen days in summer

Monday 29th June

The announcement was made; it's what we'd all been longing to hear: they weren't getting down the road! That's what they told us on the Monday, but it's still a long time to go until Sunday.

The whole week I wondered what would happen come Saturday night. I was remembering last year, when in the early hours of the Sunday morning, under the cover of darkness, the security forces descended upon us.

I was at the peace camp when they came. They did a trial run with the platoon of soldiers coming over the top of Ballyoran Hill and down on to the Garvaghy Road; suddenly they turned and went up Drumcree Road! The second time they did the same; only this time it was for real. The police in their black riot gear were tucked in behind them and they came at us with a vengeance. There was not a hope in hell that we were going to have the chance to hold a peaceful protest; they came with batons raised and boy did they use them!

I tried to convince myself this year would be different. We had the law on our side; what about the Good Friday Agreement? Surely after all the hype and talk about equality, they couldn't be seen across the world beating nationalists off the road again! The fear was in me like it was in every one else; the doubt was always there that the government would give in once again to the Orange card.

Sunday 28th June

There was a notice in the Parish Bulletin that a meeting of concerned women was to be held in the Drumcree Centre that evening.

I decided I would go to the meeting. I was disappointed that only a small number turned out – less than 25. I found the meeting to be very productive. The main concern expressed was about the consumption of alcohol in the area over the next weekend. We knew there would be a heavy security presence and one fear was that trouble could be easily started. The meeting decided that a letter would be drafted, requesting all licensed premises to close early on the Saturday evening, and for them not to sell carry-outs to the young people. Over the weekend there would be a ban on drinking in the streets. The young people had all been asked to co-operate and also to refrain from drinking or gathering in the Park.

The other important topic of discussion was the women's camp. It was decided that it would run from the Thursday night until mid-day on Saturday. It was too dangerous to run it through Saturday night considering what happened last year. Women were asked to do shifts, so there would be a presence at the camp at all times. The shifts would consist of four hours during the day or all night from twelve midnight to eight in the morning. I volunteered for the Friday night shift.

At the close of the meeting it was announced that there was to be a stewards' meeting on the following Tuesday night.

Tuesday 30th June

I went along to the community centre like a lot of other people to a meeting of people who were willing to act as stewards over the coming weekend. As the week progressed the tension grew; you could almost see it in people's faces and you could certainly feel it in the air.

By Thursday, the world's media were starting to descend upon us. No matter where you went there were television crews or photographers milling about. I wondered to myself if this was a good or a bad sign. I only hoped this year that they weren't going to get their stories or pictures on the Garvaghy Road.

Friday 3rd July

I went to the camp for twelve o'clock, as promised. There were quite a few women there. They were all sitting round the fire in one large group, chatting and laughing. I was made welcome and was soon offered a cup of coffee and a sandwich. As the small hours drew in, the crowd started to dwindle but the craic seemed to get better. There were some very entertaining characters on the night shift, and the jokes told and the comments passed had us all in stitches of laughter.

In the small hours of the morning, a strange man arrived at the camp. He told us his name was 'Fingers'. He was a character from Belfast, who on the spur of the moment had decided to come up and give us his support. We were very cautious of him at first, but discrete enquires were made from other Belfast visitors and his identity was confirmed. He kept the craic going for the rest of the night, or should I say, morning.

There was a tension in the atmosphere and it seemed to be having an effect on some people's ability to sleep. People came and went throughout the night. Some came just to say hello; others would spend a while with us, enjoying the craic. The night passed swiftly and the craic had been good, but in the back of my mind I wondered what morning would bring.

Saturday 4th July

After leaving the camp I went to the Centre to find out what was happening about the stewarding. I was advised that there would be a meeting around seven o'clock that evening. As I would not be able to attend the meeting, because I was going to Mass, I advised one of the other stewards that I would be available from nine o'clock and that I had volunteered for the Ballyoran team.

As I was about to leave, Donna called me and asked me if I was still willing to have a guest. I said, 'yes', and she introduced

cars in the fields, but now you could see the fields beginning to fill up again. There were also groups of people walking out past the chapel. What I couldn't understand was why the RUC were letting them gather in such large numbers, but I reckon they thought they would be easier to control out there instead of wrecking about the town centre. Still they should have been stopping the cars from coming into the town. They had enough check points around the whole of the town to do so.

On Monday night the stewards were out again. The area was tense, but the only disturbance we had was the sound of bands playing over the loudspeakers at Drumcree. Do these bands only have one tune? *The Sash My Father Wore* seemed to be the big favourite of the night. Of course once darkness fell, we have the helicopters back again, hovering low over our area rather than over the Orangemen.

I think it was about three o'clock when we called it a night. There was practically no one on the streets, only ourselves.

Tuesday 7th July

At 6.50am, I got up with the intention of going to work. As I got up, I looked out the window and saw about twenty men coming up the Dungannon Road; a larger group was coming out of the Moy Road. All of a sudden the police started to panic. Some rushed to close the gate on the barrier and others were rushing to put on their riot gear. I went to waken Matthew. I told him something was happening outside the front door. When I returned to look out the window again, there were about a hundred men, wearing their sashes, outside the barrier.

The police in their riot gear were inside the barrier; the Orangemen were right up to the barrier on the outside. One of the Orangemen climbed the light pole in the middle of the roundabout. He had a Union Jack flag mounted on a wooden pole and he proceeded to tape the wooden pole to the light pole. I have to say he didn't do a very good job, because it started to drop almost before he got down. It was as if it was hanging its head in shame.

After about forty minutes, the police started to move towards the gate. About the same time some landrovers with reinforcements arrived from the direction of Brankins Hill. On seeing the arrival of police reinforcements, the Orangemen started to move back from the barrier. The police moved out through the gate and along with the reinforcements they formed a semi-circle round the Orangemen and walked them down the Dungannon Road. I say 'walked' because that is what they did. They gave them the kid glove treatment!

At this stage there was a build up of cars waiting to get out of the Garvaghy Road. Once the Orangemen were a short distance down the Dungannon Road, the cars were allowed to leave. This put the notion of going to work off me. I decided I would phone in telling them that our road was being blocked.

A short time later the Orangemen appeared up the Dungannon Road again. They came, and were allowed to come right up to the roundabout, where they shouted abuse at the cars leaving the Garvaghy Road. Once again the police walked them down the Dungannon Road. They were playing cat and mouse with the police and getting away with it.

The rest of the day remained pretty quiet. There were still comings and goings at Drumcree, and the groups were still walking up and down the Dungannon Road. At one stage there was a parade of women and children from the town to the church. The police escorted them.

At about five o'clock, the crowd of Orangemen once again gathered at the roundabout. The police, when asked why they were not moving them, said that they were entitled to a peaceful protest so long as they didn't block the road. The gates had once again been closed! This was more worrying than this morning, because people would now be coming in from their work and were likely to get caught up in this crowd. The other thing that worried me was the number of people from our area that were gathering. Some of them were angry that the Orangemen weren't being moved; others were concerned about relatives who would be caught outside of the barrier.

A small white lorry approached the roundabout indicating that it wanted to come into the Garvaghy Road. As soon as the Orangemen saw it they all moved towards it, shouting abuse and banging on its sides. I also think that they broke one of his wing mirrors. The driver didn't stop! He headed towards the gates, which the police opened, and let him in. An RTE2 van was also passing through the roundabout heading down the Dungannon Road. Again the crowd surrounded it and nearly turned it on its side. Another car coming from the Dungannon Road didn't slow down for the crowd at all. They had to jump out of its way! He told me later that a soldier down the road had told him what was going on, but said he should proceed and "not stop for the f—s".

On seeing the way things were going, and I believe, partly due to the number of international observers that were now watching, the police did go out and moved them down the Dungannon Road. My brother had been caught outside and he could tell tell us that the same thing was happening down at the lower end of the road.

There was a stewards' meeting again this evening. It was decided that we would continue to patrol the area, as our presence appeared to be having a positive effect in that there had been no incidents reported that involved people from this area.

As we were leaving the Centre a crowd was gathering outside. Tension seemed to be high. When I asked what was going on, I was told that Seamus Mallon was down for a meeting. People around had got the impression that we were here because of some kind of deal to let the Orangemen down the road. As the word spread and the crowd got bigger, the tension got higher. We left that area before the meeting was over. While we were patrolling around the top end of Ballyoran, where the television crews were based, we saw on one of the monitors in the vans the reaction Seamus Mallon got on leaving the meeting.

Again we had a quiet night in the area, except for the bands, fireworks and of course the ever-hovering helicopters. The highlight of the night was when a soldier approached us, and asked if we wanted a white rabbit. They had found it on Ballyoran Hill!

Wednesday 8th July

There were no roadblocks when I got up this morning so I decided I would go to work in the Craigavon office. I could feel the tension, but I wasn't surprised, as most of the workers there would be supportive of the Orangemen.

At the stewards' meeting that evening we could see that the numbers were down. This was due to some people having gone on holidays and others having to return to work. It was decided that due to reduced numbers we would concentrate on the 'flash point' areas. These would consist of the Drumcree Road, Woodside, Garvaghy, the chapel and the Tunnel. Just before the meeting had ended, word came in that crowds were gathering up at the chapel.

Our team was covering the chapel area, so we went straight to the chapel. When we got there we found that there was a large crowd getting ready for a band parade. They were lining up on the Dungannon Road. There were cars parked all along the Dungannon and Moy Roads. The crowd on our side of the barrier was also getting bigger. They had their parade from the chapel out to the church. There was much verbal abuse towards us, but no one from our side reacted. There was a total co-operation between our people and the stewards. At one stage when we asked the people to move back to the other side of the road at Alexander Avenue just in case anything was thrown up towards us, the police and army got a little panicky. They wondered what was happening. Later one of the policemen asked me what the white arm bands were for and what were we doing. I told him that we were stewards and that we were watching his back for him. He said he was 'impressed with the co-operation we were receiving'.

The rest of the night was quiet inside the barriers. Up in the fields around the Church, there were lots of bangs; some people said they were fireworks; others thought they were blast bombs.

There was lots of shouting and cheering. Reports were filtering through that there was rioting at the Church and that they were trying to get through the razor wire fences. The whole area was very tense. The helicopters were up hovering again so there was no point in going to bed; we stayed out until it was daylight.

Thursday 9th July

I didn't bother going to work to day. I got up about around eleven o'clock and noticed that there seemed to be a lot more security forces about. I thought something had happened while I was asleep, but was told nothing had happened. As the afternoon went on, the activity increased. Helicopters were landing in the chapel carpark and in the fields behind the graveyard. At one stage there were four down in the field and two in the carpark. They were dropping off soldiers and police in their riot gear. There must have been hundreds of them dropped. I heard they were also dropping in police down at the Garvaghy dump. I wondered what was going on and if they were going to let them through after all.

As evening drew on, once again the crowds started to gather at the chapel. We had been told at the stewards' meeting that the Belfast lodges were to pay a visit that night. We knew this could be big trouble. The crowd was gathering on both sides of the barrier at the chapel. We were heavily outnumbered. Reports reckoned there were about 20,000 Orangemen. They all headed out the Dungannon Road where they regrouped and paraded in and around the roundabout. The tension was very high. Some people were scared at the numbers that were parading. The bands played as hard as they could when they reached the roundabout. On two occasions the band played *God Save the Queen* at the roundabout. All our people sat down. One onlooker said you would think it had been organised. The people went down like a domino effect. Once again all credit must be given to the residents. Throughout all the flag waving and abuse that was shouted, no reaction was given.

We could hear the shouts and blasts coming from the church. The police told us there was heavy rioting at the church and that there had been reports of shots being fired at the police at the bottom of the graveyard. Breandán had also got reports of the shooting. He said we should move everyone out of the line of fire, and up towards Jones' shop. People started to disperse when we told them what was happening. The noise of the rioting continued into the early hours.

When things had quietened down the stewards moved backed down to the house where we sat on the steps and kept watch. On a few occasions, some of the Orangemen coming back from the Church approached the barrier. When the police stopped them, they gave them verbal abuse. We had been watching and the police knew we were watching them. At one stage two men came up the road and the police let them in. We watched them proceed along the road. One appeared to be apprehensive and the other was encouraging him to go along with him. When two of the stewards moved to approach them, the police quickly ran after them and brought them back outside the barrier. One of the policemen came to us and told us that they had said they had lived in the area. We advised him that no one from this area would be coming up that road. There were no further incidents the rest of the night.

Sunday 12th July

When I got up and heard the news about the three Quinn children I couldn't believe it. It was only when I saw their photographs that it really struck me. All I could do was cry. I have asked myself many times were we to blame for their deaths. To date I haven't been able to answer. I took strength from their mother, when she said, 'The Orangemen should never get down the Garvaghy Road.'

Bernie

15

Drumcree Reminds Me of Darren

Of all the Julys, the one I will always remember most is July 1996. I remember a beautiful Wednesday evening in the back garden with my children. I had just mowed the lawn and there was a lovely smell of freshly cut grass. Despite the noise coming from the Corcrain Road I felt safe there and I knew my kids were safe with me. The noise was of bands and shouting and cheering, and car horns blowing. I turned the radio up full and let the kids shout and scream as much as they wanted so that they wouldn't be frightened or looking out to see what was going on. I wouldn't usually let them be so loud. All the time this was going on I was wondering what would happen. I was afraid of what might happen. I was afraid we would all be burned out of the estate or beaten to death but I tried to act as normal as I could. I didn't want the kids to see how afraid I was and I didn't want them to hear the anger or the hatred of the Orangemen on the Corcrain Road. I wanted to protect them from it all.

As the evening wore on, I tried to get the kids settled into bed without them knowing what was going on outside and how afraid I was, but my oldest daughter and son seemed to know already. She was only 14 that year and he was just 11 but they both started to take over getting the younger ones settled and they were being all grown-up and protective. As it got darker outside I grew more and more fearful. I got so bad, I thought I was having a nervous breakdown. I was so afraid and helpless, I wanted my own mammy to be there; I felt like I was just seven years old myself.

Around half eleven the Orangemen came back from Drumcree and I thought they might break through the police lines and attack our houses. When I was out getting my older kids in earlier on that day I asked a policeman if he thought we would be safe that night and he said, 'If they break through, there is nothing I can do to hold them back'. That kept going through my head all night. My two eldest were trying to reassure me. They said, 'We won't be killed, mammy'. I knew they were afraid too but they were putting a brave face on. They stayed up with me for hours.

It must have been six o'clock the next morning before any of us went to sleep but I was up again about half nine. It was a lovely morning and I went to the local shop on the Garvaghy Road for bread and milk. That was when I made up my mind to take my family out of Portadown to somewhere safe. I didn't know where we would go but I felt good about it. When I was walking back the police came swarming into the area and I ran out to the road to see what was happening. I saw people sitting in the middle of the road. As I walked down to them I started to feel dull and dreary. Then a very scary feeling came over me when I saw a man sitting with blood coming from his head. I saw women pleading with their sons and their husbands or brothers. They were begging them to get up and to get off the road and come home. The anguish in their faces frightened me and I ran home saying, 'Thank God my children didn't see that'. I knew then that the Orangmen were getting down the road.

I watched the evening news with my son Darren. He was 11 years old then. The Drumcree issue had already started to affect him. For three days he had talked to the police at the bottom of the street. He laughed and joked with them and he even ran errands for them. But when he saw them on the TV in their riot gear hitting people sitting on the road, he couldn't accept what he saw. He was shocked watching people covered in blood.

From that moment onwards his innocent mind was annoyed with what he had seen. I think that was the 11th of July in 1996 and from then on the sectarian war caught up with Darren. I had noticed a change in him as he became more aware of what was happening around the town. He was afraid to go to the swimming pool in town and when he said he hated Protestants because of Drumcree, I tried to tell him not all Protestants were bad.

Darren was supposed to start his first year at Drumcree College in September and I was planning for a holiday away the next summer. I didn't know it would be the last weekend of his life the weekend we went to a car boot sale. He loved going to them. He asked me was it a Protestant car boot sale and I told him it was safe. He bought himself a 'body alarm'.

I asked him what he bought the 'body alarm' for and he said really sincerely that it was to protect him from the Protestant boys. Protestant kids used to taunt the Catholics, laughing 'Ha-ha! your mas and das got beat off the road', and there was fighting every night between the Protestant and the Catholic kids over around Corcrain Orange hall. It was only when I asked him what the 'body alarm' was for that he told me about the Protestant boys calling him 'the Fenian nigger' when he went to the swimming pool in the town. Darren's daddy is black. I never really realised how bad it was for Darren till I heard his daddy joking with him saying, 'You're well marked now' and 'You can't go up the town because the colour of your skin will give you away'.

On Tuesday the 8th of October he arrived home from school at 3.45. The minute he reached the gable of the house he always used to shout, 'I'm home, mammy'. I wanted him to stay in and I tried to coax him and then I tried to get him to help me around the house. The boys all got stuck in and they were cracking jokes and laughing but I ended up finishing off the rooms myself and I didn't hear him saying, 'I'm away out, mammy'. It was a quarter past four when I was told Darren was lying on the Corcrain Road and he wasn't moving. He had been knocked down by a van and killed instantly. Somebody said he was running away from Protestant children. Darren lost his life 50 yards from the Orange hall. Although my son was knocked down by a van the accident happened because he was running away from the Protestant children.

I put flowers at the spot where he was killed that first year. I never did that again because I'm afraid that the Orange protesters at the Orange hall will destroy them. I will always associate his death with the Orange Order and Drumcree. It's not that I want to. That's just the way it is. It's nearly three years now since Darren died and it's only recently that I have been able to talk about what happened. A lot of things have happened after his death that I couldn't talk about before and that I tried to block out of my mind but I never really could. One of the things that distracts me most is an incident in the public toilets in the town. Somebody wrote on the walls about my son but I can hardly think about it never mind write it down here myself.

I hate the month of July. It brings back so many memories and so much pain. From July to October I feel I am constantly grieving for Darren. I wish there was no more parading and no more protesting and no more police. And most of all I wish Darren had not died for the so-called 'Drumcree cause'.

Marie Therese

16

Radio Equality

Radio Equality was set up on the Friday before the first Sunday demonstrations of Orangeism, with the intention of broadcasting 15-minute long information bulletins every two hours or so during the siege of the nationalist part of Portadown. It was intended to ease people's fears, dismiss unfounded rumours and speculation and to have an effective way of alerting people in the event that the British security forces caved in to the threat of Orange violence, once again.

Well – so much for intentions! It wasn't long before the handful of reluctant radio greenhorns, armed with two compact disks and a copy of the American Constitution, set about turning an emergency broadcast station into a full-time radio station with live and recorded interviews, DJs, agony aunts, public announcements, front line news, fax line, phone line, 'Love Line' – and any other line we could spin. Indeed it all got so out of line, we had to move to a bigger studio; and of course then the celebrities all wanted in on the act. We had Monica McWilliams, Gerard Rice, international observers, Martin McGuiness, Brendy, Gerry Adams, and even councillor Joe Duffy took the opportunity to do a bit of electioneering!

Then we had an Assembly member interviewing 'auld' IRA men and another man trying to get statements from a few younger ones. There were the lads bantering and wee Maria singing her head off and yer man who wouldn't sing in the barracks, but sang 'Around the Northway'. We had the Women's Writers' Group reading their poetry – and explaining the need for expressive language; and there was politics and sociology and religion and psychology; and the United Irishmen and local history, local place names, 'What the Papers (don't) Say'.

There were statements of support from every county in Ireland and from all over England, from France and Germany, America and Australia and South Africa – and half the countries in the world, from the Houses of Parliament and from members of the US Congress, from the Kurds and all sorts. While all this was going on, there was the constant clatter of helicopters overhead and the crack of gunfire, rockets, blast bombs and the occasional plastic bullet gun. The brethren baying for blood, and the billy boys on Buckfast beating the crap out of Lambeg drums and baring their arses behind Br'd's [Br'd Rodgers] back for the benefit of the world media.

But the best of all was just hearing local people talk about their lives, here, in 'The Orange Citadel' – 'The Hub -O-The-North' – 'The Black Hole'. Locals talking about what it really is like to be a working class Catholic in Portadown at the end of the 20th Century! Trimbletown two thousand – where you are liable to be shot or kicked to death because of your address – because you were handy, or you relaxed your guard, trusted the RUC and became an easy touch! Where wall murals and fly posters advertise bigotry and where prayer meetings and church services are used to solemnise sectarianism! Where men, women and children constantly risk being ridiculed, insulted and harassed if they leave their ghetto to shop or socialise! A town that is described as the 'home of Orange culture' and the 'Protestant heartland' by 'born agains' and Paisleyites! Where going to work can be 'going to Coventry' and earning a living can mean enduring the psychological torture of the silent treatment, ostracised within a factory for forty hours a week, marginalized and shunned for the 'Glorious Twelfth fortnight' – if you're lucky – and all bloody year if you're not! A town where you bite your lip, swallow your pride, and choke back your indignation at being treated like dirt rather than lose your job or get a beating, and maybe get dragged off to Edward

Street while you're still trying to figure out what you did wrong. 'Portedown' where the local Orange paper never misses an opportunity to malign your community or your elected representatives – and demonstrates its notion of inclusiveness by placing school photographs of your children among double page spreads of the self-righteous bigots who lay siege to your ghetto and have you beaten off your streets so they can demonstrate their civil and religious supremacy.

We are well used to seeing and hearing our community misrepresented by sectarian mouthpieces and the type of shallow journalism that refers to the victims of sectarianism as 'intransigent residents' groups' because they stubbornly reject demonstrations of sectarianism in their neighbourhood. I wonder is that why Radio Equality took off and seems to have been so well received (by those who could receive it) – because it was a spontaneous, uncensored moment in which to share our experiences of what it is to be a 'taig', a 'dog', a Catholic living in the birthplace and stronghold of the 'culture ' of Orangeism.

Peter

17

Radio Equality: 'In the Eye of the Storm' Broadcast on Saturday 11th July, 1998

Teresa: Just a year ago, everybody saw the police battering people off the road and now, at this very minute, they are outside our window – supposedly protecting us. How do we know, or better still, how are our children to know whether they are here to protect us or to attack us?

Joanna: My five year old thinks there are two different police forces. When she sees the rioting on TV she says, 'Oh mammy, they're awful bad'. But the other day when we were coming into the area through one of their barricades, we were stopped by a policeman looking for identification papers. Now this policeman had a face; he wasn't covered up in mask and helmet and all, and (laugh) he was very attractive and pleasant, chatty and waving at the kids in the back of the car. As we drove away, my wee girl says, 'Well, that was a nice policeman, mammy'. So now there's 'nice policemen' and 'bad policemen' – it must be an awful hard thing for children to figure out.

Teresa: When they are all togged out and have their visors down they're not human anymore – they're like robots – like what do you call it – like Robocop.

Eilish: Yes, if you can't see somebody's face, it's just so scary.

Teresa: You were saying you took your children away last July – to Donegal was it?

Joanna: Aye, but you know, taking your family away doesn't change things much. We were always listening to the car radio or going into pubs just to catch the news on TV. Our whole holiday was dominated by it. You just can't let it go. And I think what was most frightening for my children was when they saw people they knew on the TV being battered and trailed off the road by the police. Normally you can tell kids the violence on TV is not for real, that it's only a film and that it doesn't really happen. But they were watching people they knew on the streets and you couldn't tell them that.

Teresa: Do your kids ask you what was happening?

Joanna: They do – but I mean how do you explain it to anybody when you can't explain it to yourself? My wee girl is nearly five and she takes everything in. We live a bit away from the road and last year it took us a while to realise the police were moving in. When we did catch on we couldn't get to the road – soldiers invaded the whole estate and they wouldn't let us move around. She woke up and came toddling down the garden path and started pulling at me and saying, 'Come on in mammy, come on in mammy'. She wasn't happy till I closed the door and put on a video for her – as long as I was in and we couldn't hear what was happening, she thought we were safe. Then a day or so later, when we were driving past some Saracens, she immediately said, 'I'm sick mammy, I want to go home mammy'. But the minute we were away from them she said, 'I'm all-better now mammy'. She often talks about it; it's as if she's trying to sort it out in her head.

Eilish: My seven year old is petrified of the police. He saw a funeral coming one day and ran into the house and stood behind his daddy and said, 'They're coming – there's a march coming'. It took us a while to catch on what was happening, but you should have seen the relief in his wee face when we told him it was only a funeral.

Joanna: Some of the kids are hyper; they have so much energy and they have no outlet; but some others just go quiet.

Eilish: And they are always afraid something will happen when you are not in the house.

Phyllis: It's even worse this year because of the uncertainty – because you don't know what's going to happen. I haven't been sleeping or eating all week. And I'm drinking coffee and chain smoking. My whole routine is gone.

Joanna: In '97 there was a deadline but this year we don't know how long it's going to go on.

Andrea: And you can't go anywhere – there is nowhere to go.

Phyllis: Our girl is 19 and she wanted to go away for the weekend with her boyfriend but we didn't want her to go – for fear she wouldn't be able to get back in or that something would happen to her when she was out and we couldn't get to her.

Eilish: At this stage I feel like we are prisoners

(Chorus of agreement)

Phyllis: It's like a war zone. It's like something you'd see on TV.

Teresa: Somebody said it's like living in the eye of the storm.

(Chorus – 'Exactly, that's it')

Joanna: Aye – things are sort of going on relatively calmly but you're so tense. When I'm at home, I want to be at the community centre and when I'm there, I want to be at home. And at night I tell myself to go to bed but then I think there might be something on the news and it goes on like that till three or four in the morning.

Eilish: Yes – and every wee noise you hear you're up and out at the door.

Teresa: Last night I noticed there were a lot of people just walking around and I realised that that is their way of dealing with this. When you're at home, you can't switch off.

Andrea: I tried getting stuck into the housework. I had ignored it all week, waiting for them to come down the road. Then the children are under your feet all the time and you can't let them out of your sight – not even out of the Square because the police will be starting on them.

Joanna: But you know there are good things about all this. It has really developed a sense of community in the area.

Teresa: Yes.

Phyllis: Totally.

Joanna: Really and truly, just everybody is out and helping and watching out for each other.

Phyllis: More so than ever, everybody is totally together.

Teresa: That has been growing now this past three years. I heard somebody on TV saying Brendy was a bit of a cowboy – that he didn't represent the people of the area, that he only represented himself.

Phyllis: Sure we voted for him. And there's nobody could do it as good as him. And I haven't come across one person who said otherwise.

Teresa: What do you think of the general media coverage?

Andrea: They're playing it all down

Phyllis: There's so much they're not putting across.

Joanna: Yes, like what we have to live with – the fireworks and explosions, and the helicopters all through the night last night. And then some journalist said the trouble wasn't as bad last night. They want to come and sit in my house at night. It mightn't have been as bad wherever he was but it certainly was here. They don't report what it's like to live here.

Phyllis: Then some of them make out it's Brendy and the residents is the bogeymen.

Andrea: And then there's people suggesting we should be good and generous people and let them march. But sure we did that one year and look what we got for it.

Joanna: The only way the Orangemen can accept that we exist is to talk to us.

Teresa: And, I mean, there is an awful arrogance in not speaking to the people here.

Phyllis: Nobody in their right mind would say they didn't want peace – but how is it ever going to come about if the Orangemen won't speak to us?

Andrea: They're going to bully their way into getting down here. They think if they keep this going on and more wrecking that they'll get their own way.

Phyllis: The Orangemen, the way they put themselves across is they have to domineer people and make little of people who are just as good and as equal as them – but they can't accept that. They don't want to accept that.

Teresa: I wonder have we changed. Like, why has this only happened now; what changed us?

Phyllis: Speaking as the oldest person here, I'd say it's that we are better educated now.

Joanna: But we don't want to be equal in just some ways, ways that suit them. We want to be equal in every way. What we want is respect and I think they just don't want to give up their domination of us.

Teresa: Education and better jobs help people to have better self-esteem and then they want to express their needs. We have grown personally and as a community, not just in Portadown, but everywhere.

Andrea: People haven't as much fear now about speaking out.

Joanna: I was brought up in Redmanville, a Protestant estate near Corcrain, and we always felt our Protestant neighbours were our benefactors. Nothing was ever said but that feeling was there. Now I work with Protestant people and when they talk about Drumcree, it's all such a laugh to them, like it's all a huge joke. And they'd say they hoped I wasn't on the road and I sat there and said nothing. I was boiling inside but I stayed quiet. I asked myself later why I didn't say something. I think it was because we were brought up never to speak our minds in front of Protestants. The younger ones are not so afraid to speak their minds now.

Andrea: It has only been in this last few years that I have come out to protest. That's because I no longer work with Protestants.

Joanna: I think it's partly because we are having a cultural revival; I think that's why we are stronger.

Visiting American Researcher: Listening to this dialogue session for the last half hour, the question I would like to ask is, you have mentioned several times that you are afraid and I'm curious as to what you are afraid of. What does this fear mean? Are you afraid of physical attack or are you afraid that you might lose dignity in this conflict; are you afraid for your community? Could you elaborate on this expression of fear?

Joanna: It's like any form of abuse – it's the repetitiveness of it that hurts so much. As for dignity, well we have dignity; we proved that over the years when we acted peacefully and did nothing to shame ourselves. My fear is for my children. I grew up feeling a lesser person, an inferior person in my own town, and I don't want them growing up that way. I have three intelligent children and I don't want them to go through life with a good education and still feel that sense of inferiority, like I did.

Visiting researcher: What would be some potential ways in which this stand-off could be resolved and what would be the psychological impact if any of these various scenarios took place? Say, for example, that the present position stands and they are not allowed up the road, and violence breaks out; what would be the impact on your children if some compromise is reached that allows a smaller group to march? What types of solutions are out there and how do you see them affecting you and your children?

Teresa: If they get down, well, we will feel like victims again. I work with children who have been abused, physically and sexually, and often people ask why the children didn't tell. They are the victims but they don't tell on the adult abusers because they look up to and trust adults. When the abuse happens, that trust is broken, but often the abuser is someone other adults respect and trust, so the child can only think they themselves are the ones that are at fault, that they are to blame.

Andrea: Yes, we are being made to feel guilty and that just isn't right.

Teresa: That's right. But guilt can be relieved when the victim speaks out and that's what this community is doing, telling the world what has happened here. And if that is ignored and the Orangemen are allowed to go on abusing us, then they we will go on having a sense of inferiority.

Visiting researcher: But what if you took a more proactive step? You say you want the world to know what they have done to you and that it is no longer acceptable. They've hurt your community, but what if you said you would solve it without violence, wouldn't you be gaining the upper hand?

Teresa: That would be an ideal scenario – if our community could say, 'Right, OK, we'll let you walk, but you must thank us and say you won't walk'. That might save everybody's dignity – but that simply isn't going to happen because we did that in '95 and they lied and called it a victory – they used it to abuse us again.

Visiting researcher: Isn't there some compromise that can be reached so that neither side feels they have lost?

Joanna: The people here are willing to compromise. The GRRC has said it is not inconceivable that an Orange march will come down the road again – but they have to talk to us. That's the crux of the matter.

Teresa: That's the greatest insult to the people of this area, because it's an attempt to keep us marginalized and inferior; it's demeaning. And that takes us back to the abused child analogy, only here it's the British government and society that is abusing us, by backing up the abusers, by giving them status and credibility.

Joanna: The government should recognise that the majority of people here voted for the new Assembly and that the people at Drumcree voted against it. If they force them down the Garvaghy Road, then they will be betraying the people who want a settlement.

Teresa: If the Orangemen are forced through, then how is anybody going to sit down in any new forum?

Andrea: Why can't they just talk to us?

Teresa: They are not even being prevented from marching, that's what makes it all so ridiculous.

Phyllis: Why do they insist on going down the Garvaghy Road? What is the logic of it?

Visiting researcher: Can you imagine that in any way at all they are afraid?

Joanna: Yes, afraid of losing their grip on society in Northern Ireland; that's why they feel threatened.

Visiting researcher: In periods of change people do react in very radical ways, because they are clinging onto things in a desperate way; that's what I see happening.

Andrea: They are afraid of Catholics being equal to them.

Phyllis: It's fear of the unknown, about their future.

Visiting researcher: They know there's a new situation out there, but they don't know what awaits them.

Phyllis: What I see is equality for everyone and that's bound to be a good thing.

Visiting researcher: This reminds me of the civil rights movement in the USA when it was agreed that blacks would have rights to go to school, etc. The white population felt that they had a lot to lose. It took a great amount of convincing that they wouldn't lose anything, and within about ten years it was over. The Civil Rights movement achieved its objective and we don't see this type of violence anymore. I feel however it's very important that each side be sympathetic towards one another and these issues can sometimes be dealt with much quicker.

Teresa: That's why dialogue is so important, so we can understand each other's fears. We will only get to know each other's fears and expectations through dialogue.

18
Radio Equality:
12th July, Live Broadcast

Helen: No-one could wake up to this morning's news of the three children being burned to death in Ballymoney and not be deeply affected. But imagine how our children must feel when they hear about it. I find it very difficult to explain something like that to my children. You see, with all that's going on around us here in Garvaghy, the only place they feel safe is in their home. And then for them to hear about them three children being burned to death in their beds – how can anybody explain that depth of hostility and brutality?

Sharon: It's like... My 12 year old daughter was a friend of little Darren Murray's; he was knocked down near his home as he ran away from a gang of young loyalists. It was in the school holidays, around this time of the year. Within minutes of him being knocked down, she came into the house literally squealing about him being run over. He died after a few days on a life support machine and when the news came through he was dead, she cried and cried. Even months later when she was going back to school, she said, 'If Darren was alive, he would be starting first class at the new school with us'. Darren lived near the school and he was knocked down running home for safety. She doesn't always talk about him, but only a week or so ago she said, 'It's hard to believe he's dead'. Drumcree will always remind her of him. He was killed because of Drumcree too.

Helen: People tend to assume that when things get back to a bit of so-called normality here that it's all over and done with for the children, but it has lasting affects on them.

99

Denice: My daughter is staying with relatives in England this year – because she's afraid. She stayed here through it all last year, but this year she just couldn't wait to get away. She said she was afraid some of us would be killed if Drumcree happened again this year. They never forget about it; they talk among themselves about it.

Denice: I have a 17 year old son and he won't even go out of the house; (crying) he just sits in all the time and...

Helen: Ah, don't cry; it's hard, I know, it's very sad. I think the children who withdraw have the hardest time dealing with it all.

Denice: I think the children are feeling hurt but they won't show it in front of their parents in case they make them feel bitter and go out and get involved.

Helen: What age is your son?

Denice: He's 17 and he sits in all the time. It's the only place he feels safe. I moved into Woodside a lock of years ago, to get away from the road, and he was so happy. But then the trouble started in the Bann fields, just behind Woodside. Protestant children, and men too, started coming over the fields to attack the area and he was nearly hysterical. He wasn't sleeping and I had to stay home constantly reassuring him that nobody was going to touch him. He couldn't believe they could come so close to the house. Then there was a security barrier put up and I could see that he felt better, got a wee bit of confidence again. Then, this morning when we heard about Ballymoney I could see it in his face, in his eyes, the fear.

Helen: Yes, it's very sad. Parents are at a loss as to what to do. I know of a woman who phoned the psychiatric services for her child because he was becoming so aggressive; it was the tension during the siege last year. They said they had a waiting list and she said, 'But I can't wait'. It's worse for the younger children who can't articulate their feelings, the four and five year olds. If we have difficulty dealing with what's happening what must it be like for them?

Sharon: I have a nine year old, profoundly deaf child. He has a very good friend who lives in the Protestant side of town and they spend a lot of time together; he's deaf too. Now he knows there's things going on but how do you explain to him that he can't go to stay at his friend's house? He has me tortured asking, 'Please mammy – even just for an hour'. It's the same for his friend's mum. They get on great together and communicate really well. But now he's isolated and they are cut off completely. His friend's mum is too afraid to come in here – that's understandable. And I wouldn't take my child to her area now. Last week, she was bringing my child home and she was stopped at a roadblock and asked where she was going. When she said she was bringing my son home to the Garvaghy Road the policemen advised her to get him home quickly. But she got afraid to come in and phoned us to go for him. We don't have the special phones and now the children can't communicate. He feels he has lost his only friend.

Helen: How are we going to build bridges between our two communities with this going on, and make a future for our children?

Denice: This hasn't just been happening for four or five years. I sent my children to the mixed school so they would be growing up and not caring about differences between Protestants and Catholics. I thought I was doing the right thing, but then at 11 or 12, they were too old for the mixed school and had to move on, and they couldn't meet their Protestant friends anymore. When one of them was 17, he got a job in the town and one of his Protestant school-friends was there – but he wouldn't let on he knew my son in front of other Protestant workers; he wouldn't show any friendship. My son just couldn't believe it; he said he wanted to talk to him, 'but he didn't want to know me'. That hurt him and he said, 'Well, if he doesn't want to talk to me when his friends are around, then I don't think I'll bother. I don't want to talk to him.' The fella would only talk to him when they were alone together, but it was back to the cold shoulder when there were any Protestants around. It's hard for him to realise that they are under more pressure than we are, that we have nothing to lose by being friendly with them but they have. They have more fear of that than our children have.

Helen: Where does their fear come from?

Denice: From their parents maybe. Or maybe from groups bullying, I really don't know. Maybe it's just older friends that say, 'Don't you be talking to him'. As soon as you walk into a place, they know you and you can feel the fear and the tension in the place. But you do your best to get along and build some kind of friendship – just because you need a job, to support your family. They're OK maybe on a one-to-one basis – but they're always looking round them to see if anybody is watching them talking to you or having a laugh. It's OK if they're asking you about something about work – 'would you do that or this?' – but they won't come into a close friendship with you.

Helen: Some parents say their children won't even go up the town. How can we get Catholic and Protestant children together?

Sharon: I think the way to do that is to get our children to understand that not all Protestants belong to the Orange Order and that there's good and bad in everybody. Our children have become so bitter after watching their brothers, sisters, mothers, and fathers being beaten and they need to know that not everybody is like the people in the field.

Helen: More integrated education and youth clubs then?

Denice: But the children move on, out into the workplaces, and you still have the older generation and they won't let go; they keep the children apart. The murder of those three children in their house has brought so much fear. What's going to happen next?

Helen: The problem is when we tell our children that not all Protestants are like the ones at Drumcree, we also have to teach them that, for their own safety, they have to be wary, to remember what happened to Robbie Hamill. And all the other things that have happened here.

Denice: The Orangemen say it's just a ten-minute walk, but children in this area are on their guard twelve months of the year; that's why I feel so much for them. They're living in fear. The older ones can't even enjoy a night out for worrying about getting home.

Sharon: It's 52 weeks of the year that goes on and then the police taunt them too. They are constantly harassing the teenagers. So you tell them to be wary of strangers and you tell them to be wary of the police – there's no logic in it.

Helen: If we are to teach our children anything shouldn't it be that we are not second class citizens, that we are not inferior, that we have nothing to be ashamed of? But then it's only if we change ourselves that we can ever teach our children to challenge the bigots who treat us as inferior people.

Denice: I think a lot of parents try to live their lives over again through their children and they encourage them to stand up for themselves.

Helen: It seems to me that what this whole Garvaghy Road thing symbolises is something people find hard to explain to their children; it's that we want to give people back their dignity and encourage that in our children. It's like, people are saying, 'Why can't they let them down the road, it's just a 15 minute walk' and all that sort of thing. But it really does represent what you said – we have to be listened to, our wishes have to be respected. This must work for us this time – we are at the point now when we are saying, 'It's now or never; we're not going to go back to how it was, to being second class citizens.' I don't want to be doing this, and I don't want my children to be doing this in 20 years' time. Our parents weren't able to do it for us – but history takes its course and this is the make-or-break situation. Portadown represents the situation of Catholics all over Northern Ireland and people are looking towards us; they are identifying with the people of Garvaghy and they're expecting the governments to support us.

Denice: Yes, and our community is so much stronger, more so this year than ever before and there's no going back to being treated the way our parents were. We couldn't have done it a few years ago. Now there are good spokespeople about and this has brought us together – there's no backing down now. Unionists are going to have to understand that we'll take nothing from them but we will be treated as equals – that we want our rights as human beings.

19

The legacy of Drumcree '98

One would have to be here to experience the trauma and tension under which we lived for fourteen days, and it still goes on ten weeks later. As the weekend of July 5th approached, we were overwhelmed by the awfulness of the barbed wire, barricades, trenches, cameras, etc. which we saw being put into place.

What was most striking and horrifying was the realisation that people who professed to be Christian had to be kept apart in such a manner. How awful! The residents of the Garvaghy Road were referred to by Unionist politicians and Orangemen as 'dogs', ' monsters', 'animals' and 'scum of the earth'. When I heard Breandán Mac Cionnaith take issue with these men for speaking of us in such an offensive and degrading manner, I shed tears of hurt and anger, and wondered about a future for nationalists in Portadown. As we wandered round the enclosed area of the Garvaghy Road, the whole set-up did give the impression of wild animals being caged in and kept apart. It was very difficult and painful to live in such an inhuman situation.

The barricades and the fear of loyalist protests prevented people from moving freely or going into town and going about their normal business. When family members were prevented from going to their places of work, tension and anger often erupted in their homes. There was an eerie silence in the area – the voices of children were seldom heard as parents kept them indoors for safety. Real fear and a lack of trust in the police and in the British government gripped the people in an inordinate way from time to time. The betrayal which they experienced over the past three years when the parades were forced down the Garvaghy Road will not be easily forgotten. This was obvious when Seamus Mallon arrived in the area. Straight away the fear of a 'sell-out' and being subjected to another forced parade was too much to even contemplate. There was a constant swing in the mood of the community.

As I stated above, family life was under great strain and stress. 'They'll get down,' I heard the father of the house say; the next moment an explosion of rage erupted at the prospect. All may have been calm and peaceful on the Garvaghy Road, as portrayed in the media, but there was tangible strain and trauma when one entered the homes of many of the residents. As tension and fear was mounting, a call came from the people to come together and pray for a just and peaceful resolution. It was responded to immediately. This time of coming together proved to be a great comfort and support to those people, especially the women and children who felt powerless in the situation. Many of them were locked in their homes all day listening to the news and watching the latest bulletin on the TV. 'I love meeting the people before the night sets in and having the chat', said Teresa. 'I know in my heart that good will come from this terrible situation we are in', said Mary. 'Our prayers won't go astray.' Frances from Yorkshire said she came to Northern Ireland to pray for all Ulster. All who came felt welcome, and left with a little more hope and love in their hearts.

Sunday morning, July 12th, dawned with the news of the terrible murders of Richard, Mark and Jason Quinn, all burned in a petrol bomb attack on their home. We were all in total shock. Men women and children spent the early hours of the morning crying quietly in their homes. Some wept with feelings of guilt, others for the grieving mother who heard the last cries of her dying children: 'I'm here in the corner, mummy', and 'I can't see the stairs.' Then the whole place went up in flames. No doubt Christine Quinn will hear the cries of her children ringing in her ears until she joins her little ones some day.

We will never forget Drumcree 1998. As I said in some way our community felt guilty because of the deaths of the three children. All we heard was, 'We knew something drastic would happen, but we never thought three wee ones would be the victims.' This terrible tragedy was a turning point in the events of the Drumcree stand-off. All of a sudden, people were brought to their senses. 'No march is worth a life', said Reverend Bingham, and called on the Orange Order to leave Drumcree. This statement encouraged other ministers to take a stand against the behaviour of the Orangemen, many of whom responded by withdrawing their support.

Our community was also very encouraged by the presence of Archbishop Brady at all masses on the Sunday. Many hours have been spent mulling over the happenings of the last three weeks. As we conclude our sharings on Drumcree 1998, we are convinced that the deaths of the little Quinn boys will not be in vain. Good will eventually come from the great tragedy. We must continue by our prayers and love to support their mum, dad and their surviving brother.

Laura

Hate literature distributed by loyalists after Rosemary Nelson's murder. Sections blanked out are so grossly offensive that the publishers have refused to reproduce them

MONSTER MASHED

In the famous film "The Wizard of Oz", there is a point where the Munchkins dance around singing the "The Wicked Witch is Dead".

Throughout Ulster similar scenes of joy were repeated as loyalists heard of the death of civil rights abuser Rosemary Nelson. *Red Hand* has never, of course, taken any satisfaction from the death of anyone as we regard all Her Majesty's subjects in Ulster as having the potential to become loyalists.

In the aftermath of her untimely demise the liberal media has sought to portray Nelson as a "human rights lawyer" - nothing could be further from the truth. She was in fact a human rights abuser.

Nelson was a prominent player in the IRA's murder machine by acting as their "house lawyer" - providing vital services to the Provo death squads

IRA lawyer Rosemary Nelson

Setting up her legal office in Lurgan she quickly became a vital cog in the Mid-Ulster Provo death machine. She became the Provos' house lawyer for the area - constantly on call to visit arrested scum and seeking to undermine cases by inventing complaints against RUC and UDR men. In addition, her access to confidential court files allowed her to identify members of the security forces, IRA informers and loyalists for the Provo death squads.

More sinister still was her participation in IRA anti-interrogation techniques where she advised scum on how to act whilst in police custody. Whatever else she may have been, Nelson was intelligent and knew how to prepare her clients both before and after the murders they committed. Since 1984 nobody has been successfully prosecuted for the 14 murders committed by republicans in Lurgan town - that is the 'success' Rosemary Nelson helped secure for her clients.

Her most high profile client was Lurgan mass murderer Colin Duffy *(pictured, right)* - the main IRA killer in the town.

Sharing a physical disability (one of Duffy's legs is an inch shorter than the other) brought the Gruesome Twosome closer together than is normal for client and lawyer. Indeed, Duffy was

In doing so he displayed rather more courage than he did in performing his cowardly murders of innocent Protestants.

In the last two years Nelson had also begun to appear more and more frequently in the neighbouring town of Portadown advising Brendan McKenna and his crew on how best to ethnically cleanse Protestants from the town.

It is of course sad that anyone has to die, especially when the prospects for peace have been so good in recent years. While we would never gloat about anyone's death, no loyalist can but feel that in this instance justice has been done.

****

COLLUSION?

A startling three-in-four republican murders remain unsolved while almost 50 per cent of all killings attributed to loyalists over the last 30 years have resulted in charges.

12

From left to right: Sinn Féin Assembly representatives Francie Molloy, Dara O'Hagan, Martin McGuinness (also MP) and local councillor Breandán Mac Cionnaith on the Garvaghy Road, July 1998

SDLP councillors Bríd Rodgers and Alex Attwood, with Deputy First Minister (designate) Seamus Mallon (also MP) confronted by residents in Churchill Park, July 1998 (see pages 5-6)

Congressman Donald Payne and Senator Tom Hayden find their way blocked by the RUC as they try to view the Orangemen's protest at Drumcree, 1997

Catholic priests are denied access to St. John's Church, 6th July 1997 (see page 165)

The 1997 invasion

Residents' block the Garvaghy Road, 1996

Open air Sunday Mass 1997 (see pages 165-6)

Top left: 1997
top right: 1997
bottom left: 1997
bottom right: 1998

Photo: Mal McCann
(far right)
An Phoblacht/RN

Photo: Kim Haughton

Rosemary Nelson
stands between
advancing RUC riot
squads and residents,
July 6th 1997 (see
page 165)

Photos: Mal McCann

Top left: RUC drag boy off father's knee

Photos: Mal McCann

Photo: Mal McCann

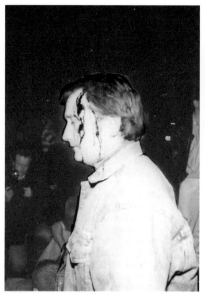

Photo: Derek Speirs/Report

Photo: Derek Speirs/Report

Photo: Mal McCann

The scenes after New Labour Secretary of State,
Mo Mowlam, pushes the 1997 Orange parade down 'the road'

29 May 1999. Residents protest against a Junior Orange
Order march in the lower end of the Garvaghy Road

PART II

'It started here; it will end here'

ORANGE MARCHES IN PORTADOWN: A NATIONALIST PERSPECTIVE

Based on an edited and updated version of a
submission made by the
Garvaghy Road Residents' Coalition to the
Independent Review of Parades and Marches
November 1996

20

'It started here; it will end here'

Orange Marches in Portadown: A Nationalist Perspective

Introduction

Portadown, County Armagh, has always been deeply divided; power and authority, civil and political rights, and access to sources of wealth have not been equally shared. It is an unpleasant reality that in housing, schools, business life, religion and in politics, Portadown is almost completely segregated. To a large degree, Portadown can be viewed as a microcosm of Northern Ireland.

Portadown is one of the largest towns in County Armagh and has a unionist/nationalist population of approximately 22,000 to 6,000. The nationalist community was historically based around the Obins Street area of the town, but now resides in the estates which sprawl along the Garvaghy Road. With the construction of schools, churches and some services and small businesses this area now has a degree of autonomy that makes it a clearly defined area resembling a small town.

While Portadown is a relatively wealthy and industrialised town, the nationalist area is one of chronic social and economic deprivation and impoverishment. Irrespective of whatever indicators of social need one cares to adopt the nationalist areas have been and still remain the areas of most intense social need within Portadown.

However the nationalist community has discovered how to address many of its needs. There has been a growth in community spirit. The residents have formed clubs and associations with the aim of servicing the social needs of their area. Between St. Mary's Youth Club, the Ashgrove Community Centre and Drumcree Community Centre there are services for play-school, crèche, youth club, disabled and handicapped, adult education, Irish culture: language classes, dance, literature; OAP services and activities. At all levels groups build links with the wider Portadown community. Sport is thriving, with several different clubs within the area. Groups have managed to attract significant funding for projects. Mayfair Business Centre and Bannside Development have brought over a million and a half pounds of investment to boost economic development.

All this voluntary activity and the co-operation with statutory bodies reflect a maturity and growing confidence of the nationalist residents. While the social deprivation means that the community suffers an excessive burden of social problems it also produces a high proportion of young adults with good education who are our hope for a better future.

One could have the impression that this is a healthy community which has dignity. This possibility is shattered each year during the 'marching season' and compounded by severe restrictions placed by the police on the right of nationalists to parade and to express their communal, national and cultural identities.

While the events of July 1995 to July 1998 have made the names of Drumcree and the Garvaghy Road echo around the world, the background to those events are often ignored in the media and by political commentators. In this presentation we will emphasise that actions by the community are a positive expression of the dignity of the people, their desire to continue to grow and ultimate desire to strive for relationships in Portadown where the dignity and rights of no one are undermined. By explaining the historical context of those events and by giving a voice to Portadown's nationalist minority, we hope to present the case why it is reasonable for the vast majority of residents of the area to demand a partial re-routing of Orange parades away from the area.

Parades in a divided society

Parades by the Orange Order and its sister organisation the Royal Black Preceptory have long proven to be a source of major controversy for the town's nationalist community. That arises from the insistence of the Orange Order and others to route some of these parades through areas which are almost exclusively nationalist. For many years, nationalists have campaigned for, and actively demanded, the re-routing of these contentious parades away from their neighbourhoods. They view the whole issue as being simple and straightforward: one that questions the morality and justice of the state authorities in permitting any parade to proceed through an area where the vast majority of residents are opposed to it.

We recognise and uphold the fundamental value of freedom of speech and expression of all people and groups in a democratic state. But Northern Ireland is a bitterly divided society with a legacy of conflict between two main communities with their distinct identities. The right of freedom of expression must be exercised: i) fairly, ii) sensitively and iii) with the minority being given due respect. In Portadown this has not been the case. i) The majority tradition has been given freedom of expression throughout the town, with an excessive number of parades and excessive displays of symbols, while the minority community is restricted to their residential area; ii) the excessive nature of the majority celebration and their demand to celebrate their political, religious and cultural identity in the residential area of the minority is blatantly insensitive to the feelings, dignity and rights of the minority community; iii) the minority have not been given space to celebrate their culture, religion or politics in a manner consistent with their number.

In a town where the nationalist population is a 6,000 minority and the unionist population is a 16,000 majority, such parades through areas which are overwhelmingly nationalist take on an added significance – the dark suspicion and belief that these parades are an attempt by the majority to stamp their influence, and indeed, their supremacy upon the minority. That suspicion is added to even further when one realises that the route of these contentious parades lies directly along a road which is the main artery, if not the very heart, of the area where the vast majority of the town's nationalist population, over 1,500 families, reside.

The chief failure has been the unwillingness of the government to restrict parades of the majority tradition, especially when they oppose the state in a structured way, and the inability of the police force to enforce the law impartially. Thus, the issue of Orange parades goes to the very heart of the northern state. In no other democratic or western society would it be conceivable that the forces of the state would force a march or parade by one ethnic, political or religious group through that of another, especially one organised by an association whose members are required to strenuously oppose the religious and political beliefs of the resident community.

The Orange Order and the Ulster Unionist Party

The Orange Order is an exclusively Protestant organisation. Claims by the Order that it is a purely religious body concerned solely with the maintenance of the Protestant faith often ring hollow in nationalist ears. The Order's often publicised and direct ties with, and influences on, the political forces of unionism are all too evident both historically and at present.

It was first established, near Portadown, at the end of the 18th century. By the 1920s and partition, the Orange Order had become the largest single bloc within the Ulster Unionist Council, the ruling body of the Ulster Unionist Party, the party which governed the Six Counties in what was in effect a one-party state until the abolition of Stormont, the northern parliament, in 1972. During the lifetime of the Stormont regime, over half of the seats held by Unionists were uncontested at elections.

These ties between the Unionist Party and the Orange Order were replicated throughout the North at local level, as a brief look at the Orange/Unionist relationship in Portadown shows.

Five of the seven men who have held the post of District Master of the Order in Portadown since partition were also prominent members of the Unionist Party. W.H.Wright, District Master until 1926, was a legal advisor to both Portadown and Lurgan town Councils, and the Secretary of North Armagh Unionist Association. He was also credited with having played a leading role in the formation of the Ulster Volunteer Force. Major David Shillington was a Unionist MP at Stormont and a Cabinet minister for several years during the 1930s and 40s. Dr. George Dougan was also a Unionist MP.

Robert Magowan was an elected representative for almost forty years, from 1926 until 1964. During that time he held the posts of Chairman of Portadown Urban Council and Mayor of Portadown Borough Council on several occasions. Magowan not only held the post of District Master but also that of County Grand Master. Herbert Whitten, District Master of the Order in Portadown from 1968–1981, was also very prominent in unionist politics. A mayor of Portadown and also of Craigavon Borough Council, Whitten was a Unionist MP as well. Other Portadown Orangemen who were leading figures in the controlling Unionist Party included Isaac Hawthorne, another MP and one time Chief Whip in the Stormont parliament. W.H.Wolsley, a leading Orangeman who became Mayor of Portadown in the 50s, was later to receive 'the compliments of LOL 89 for his services to the brethren whilst being a member of the Council'.

One Orange lodge alone, LOL 608, has provided three mayors of Portadown – Edward Cassells, Frank Dale and Alfred Martin; one mayor of Craigavon in 1994-95, Brian Maginness; and one chairman of Armagh District Council, George McCartney.

Throughout the 1970s and 80s, the Unionist-controlled Craigavon council earned notoriety as a result of being found guilty of discriminatory practices by the courts. On one occasion this led to 12 Unionist councillors, amongst whom were several well-known members of the Orange Order, being surcharged for their actions and disqualified from holding public office. The twelve were found to have been guilty of conducting a campaign of discrimination against a local Gaelic football club.

In March 1985, the then Mayor of Craigavon, Arnold Hatch, was one of the most prominent of those who prevented a St Patrick's Day parade being held by nationalists in Portadown. The former Westminster MP for Upper Bann, the late Harold McCusker, left many of his nationalist constituents in Portadown with an indelible memory with his beating of a Lambeg drum as he took part in Orange marches through their neighbourhood.

Indeed, it is no secret that the Orange Order played a major role in securing the leadership of the Ulster Unionist Party for David Trimble in 1995 following his prominent role during the stand-off at Drumcree caused by the opposition of local residents to an Orange March along the Garvaghy Road.

Furthermore, the fact that many members of the RUC are themselves members of the Orange Order, or its sister organisations, the Black Preceptory and the Apprentice Boys, calls into question their ability to behave in an impartial and unbiased manner in relation to the issue of these marches. It is believed that 25% of RUC personnel are in the Loyal Orders. A number of RUC personnel are under investigation for having participated in illegal blockades during July 1996 in support of the Portadown Orangemen at Drumcree.

This relationship between Orangeism and unionism is seen by the nationalist community to politicise parades by the Orange Order. An Orange 'church' parade cannot pretend to be merely or exclusively a religious affair and demand privileges that a society might rightly bestow to a purely religious event. It is clearly a significant political statement and therefore ought to be treated as such in the debate on freedom of expression.

Violent Clashes 1795 – 1912

> The Orange institution has been at pains to avoid confrontation and to conduct themselves with the utmost decorum as befitting a religious organisation. (Orange Order statement, July 1995)

In June 1795, a Portadown clergyman, the Rev. George Maunsell, implored his congregation to 'celebrate the anniversary of the Battle of the Boyne in the true spirit of the institution' by attending a service to be conducted by a Rev. Devine on July 1st. That July 1st service was to be the antecedent of the Orange Order's later church services at Drumcree. Francis Plowden described what happened after the Rev. Devine's service for the 'Orange boys'.

> This evangelical labourer in the vineyard of the Lord of Peace so worked up the minds of his audience, that upon retiring from service, on the different roads leading to their respective homes, they gave full scope to the anti-papistical zeal with which he had inspired them, falling upon every Catholic they met, beating and bruising them without provocation or distinction, breaking the doors and windows of their houses, and actually murdering two unoffending peasants who were digging in a bog. This unprovoked atrocity of Protestants revived and redoubled religious rancour. The flame spread and threatened a contest of extermination. (*History of Ireland*, Vol. 1, 1809.)

It was two months later, after another bloody sectarian confrontation, known as the Battle of the Diamond, in a townland near the village of Loughgall in County Armagh, that the first Orange lodge was set up and the first Orangemen sworn into membership. The Battle of the Diamond, in which 30 nationalists and no Protestants were killed, was one of the worst outrages in what historians have referred to ever since as the Armagh outrages – widespread intimidation and terror. Hundreds of families, most of them Catholics, were forced to leave their homes when threatened by armed men in the dead of night and to flee the county entirely.

At a meeting convened by the Governor of County Armagh, Lord Gosford, on December 28th 1795, thirty magistrates reached the following resolution:

> Resolved, that it appears to this meeting, that the County of Armagh is at this moment in a state of uncommon disorder, that the Roman Catholic inhabitants are grievously oppressed by lawless persons unknown, who attack and plunder their homes by night and threaten them with instant destruction,

unless they abandon immediately their lands and habitations... The only crime, which the wretched objects of this ruthless persecution are charged with, is a crime indeed of easy proof: it is simply a profession of the Roman Catholic faith, or an intimate connection with a person professing that faith...

The 'wreckers'' operations ranged from murder and arson to the destruction of crops, animals, looms and furnishings. By the end of 1796, an estimated 3,500 Catholics had been terrorised and driven out of their homes in County Armagh by this campaign of wrecking.

On July 12th, 1797, the first Grand Committee of the Orange Order was appointed at a meeting in Portadown. A report in the *Belfast News Letter* of August 21, 1812, shows vividly how widespread the Orange philosophy had become in a relatively short time. The entire Armagh Yeomanry was disbanded by the Lord Lieutenant due to 'insubordination.' The insubordination came to light on the 2nd of July when a sergeant and nine privates were dismissed for refusing to serve under an officer who had signed a petition in favour of Catholic Emancipation. 'A mutinous spirit' was then said to have become manifest amongst the Yeomanry throughout the county. As a result, the authorities were left with no other option but to disband what in fact became the Orange Order's military wing in County Armagh. Previous to their disbandment, it was commonplace for entire companies of Yeomen to take part in Orange parades wearing full ceremonial uniform.

A party of Orangemen returning from Middletown on July 12th, 1822, attacked Catholic homes at Cruskeenan and murdered a Catholic named Patrick Grimley. At the inquest five days later, it was alleged that two sons of the Rev. Nathaniel Smith, rector of Madden, and another man named Brown had attacked Grimley in his own home with swords and a pistol. Within a few months the Rev. Smith's son, Samuel, was charged with Grimley's murder. He was found not guilty.

The following year four Orangemen were tried and acquitted of the murder of a Catholic, Michael Campbell, at Killileagh in County Armagh. Campbell had been shot dead and several other Catholics wounded by Orangemen taking part in a July parade.

The activities of the Orange Order led to its attempted suppression by an Act of Parliament in 1825 chiefly because of the sectarian turmoil and disruption caused by its annual parades. The Grand Lodge of Ireland dissolved itself as a consequence of this new law. Nevertheless, on July 12th of that year, Portadown Orangemen defied the authorities and marched through the town. Magistrates unsuccessfully ordered the dispersal of the marchers but the police force available was said to have been found insufficient, and the brethren were able to march unhindered.

In July 1826, twenty-one Orangemen were charged with offences arising out of an incident at Tartaraghan on the outskirts of Portadown. Despite the evidence of eye-witnesses, including the local Catholic parish priest, Rev. Coleman, all were acquitted of the attack and destruction of a Catholic place of worship.

Portadown magistrate, Mr. C. Woodhouse, in a last minute effort to prevent an unlawful Orange parade taking place on July 12th 1827, called all the local leaders of the Orange Order together that morning. The Orangemen refused to listen to his appeal, and some 5,000 were said to have marched through the town that day.

1828 saw Orangemen in Belfast and a number of other areas abide by the wishes of the authorities: no marches took place. However, Portadown Orangemen displayed their contempt and disregard for those same authorities by parading as usual with flags flying and discharging their fire-arms. In July 1829, almost 2,000 Orangemen again defied the authorities and marched through Portadown. There was widespread rioting and shootings, with serious sectarian disturbances breaking out in Armagh, Strabane, Newtownstewart, Castlewellan, Enniskillen, Stewartstown and Maghera. One Belfast newspaper claimed that up to twenty people had been killed as a result of the disturbances. The District Master of the Order in Armagh city, Mr. G. Tyrell, was charged with having caused the riots there on July 13.

In November 1830, an Orange parade through the village of Maghery, a few miles from Portadown, resulted in most of the houses in that locality being destroyed and the inhabitants fleeing for their lives. Evidently, the Orangemen were still maintaining their policy of 'wrecking' which had proved so effective in the past. Residents of the predominantly Catholic village were to give evidence before the Parliamentary Select Committee investigation into the Orange Order in 1835.

The Party Processions Act, which was given the Royal Assent in 1832, and which was to be enforced for the next five years, was continuously defied by Portadown Orangemen. Commenting on the Act at Armagh Summer Assizes in 1833, a Judge Moore said that its objective was,

> to put an instant stop to parties marching in procession, with colours, badges, or other insignia, calculated to create a disturbance or arouse religious and political animosity in His Majesty's Roman Catholic subjects.

On July 12th, 1833, an estimated 20,000 Orangemen and their supporters paraded illegally through Portadown to Carrickblacker House, the residence of Lieutenant Colonel William Blacker, one of the most influential figures within the entire Orange Order. Fourteen Orangemen were later charged with taking part in the proceedings. The authorities in Dublin Castle who were becoming increasingly alarmed at the activities of Blacker later stripped him of his commission and dismissed him as a Justice of the Peace for County Armagh.

On the same day as the Carrickblacker demonstration, Orangemen returning from an illegal demonstration attacked the Catholic hamlet of Ballyhagan and injured a number of people. A petition complaining of the collusion of Portadown magistrates and police in preventing the prosecution of twenty-one identified members of the attackers was sent to the Marquis of Anglesey, the Lord-Lieutenant General and Governor General of Ireland. The leading Orangeman, William Blacker, was the chairman of the petty sessions at Portadown. Joseph Atkinson, who also presided over the petty sessions was not only an Orangeman but was also related to one of the accused.

Hugh Donnelly, a 29 year old Catholic from Drumcree, was killed after being struck on the head with a stone during a confrontation with Orangemen in 1835. Six out of seven

Orangemen indicted for his murder at the County Armagh Summer Assizes were found guilty on the lesser charge of manslaughter.

The behaviour of the Orangemen in general can be gauged by evidence submitted to the Parliamentary Select Committee by a County Armagh magistrate, William J. Hancock, a Protestant, in relation to July 1835 in Portadown.

> For some time past the peaceable inhabitants of the parish of Drumcree have been insulted and outraged by large bodies of Orangemen parading the highways, playing party tunes, firing shots, and using the most opprobrious epithets they could invent... A body of Orangemen, wearing Orange lilies, marched through the town ... and proceeded to Drumcree Church, passing by the Catholic chapel though it was a considerable distance out of their way... On Sunday, Monday, and Monday night, and a great deal of Tuesday, the peaceable citizens of the town were alarmed and terrified by the frequent discharge of musketry, accompanied by the most menacing language ...

Following the Select Committee in 1835 on the activities of the Orange Order, the Grand Master of the Orange Order, the Duke of Cumberland, who was in fact the King's brother, sent a letter to Prime Minister Russell stating that he would take all legal steps to have the Order dissolved. On April 13th 1836 the Grand Lodge met in Dublin and voted in favour of dissolving the Orange Institution – in accordance with the King's wishes.

Portadown Orangemen were again to demonstrate their extremism and contempt for the King to whom they supposedly professed loyalty. A meeting was held on June 13 with many influential Portadown Orangemen present. The meeting decided that since the Grand Lodge no longer existed, the County Armagh Grand Lodge would now take control of the Orange Order and William Blacker was elected the new Grand Master. In July Orangemen paraded defiantly through the town and at least 50 later appeared in court for taking part in the unlawful procession.

Nine years later, police and magistrates failed to prevent an Orange march from entering a Catholic part of Armagh City.

The march sparked of a major riot between the Orangemen, many of whom were armed, and the Catholic residents. One Catholic died and several others were injured when the Orangemen opened fire. Three Orangemen were later convicted of manslaughter and received extremely light sentences ranging from one to four months!

On July 12th, 1860 at Derrymacash, situated between Lurgan and Portadown, a total of sixteen Catholic inhabitants were shot by those taking part in the annual Orange parade; one died later. A number of Catholic homes were wrecked and the Catholic chapel attacked. No Orangemen were injured, but, subsequently, twelve of them were found guilty of taking part in the riot, and a thirteenth Orangeman was found guilty of the manslaughter of Thomas Murphy, the Catholic who died. At the inquest into Murphy's death, lawyers acting for the deceased's family unsuccessfully attempted to have members of the Orange Order barred from sitting on the jury.

The Derrymacash outrage led to the passing of an amended Party Processions Act in August 1860. The amended Act forbade the carrying of arms and wearing party colours in processions. Like previous legislation aimed at curtailing the activities of the Orange Order, it had little or no effect, particularly in County Armagh where many members of the judiciary, military and police, if not actual members of the Order, were either openly sympathetic to, or intimidated by, Orangeism.

In 1864, although no major incidents were reported in Portadown, Belfast exploded in a cycle of sectarian violence that lasted eighteen days and left 12 people dead and over 100 others seriously injured.

In September 1867, Orangemen, complete with bands and drumming parties, assembled outside St. Patrick's Catholic Church in Portadown's William Street during the annual mission retreat. People were attacked on their way to and from chapel, and one of the priests was knocked unconscious. The parish priest, Fr. Hughes, was reported to have urged the men of the parish to band together for their own protection. The RIC Sub-

Inspector for Portadown was later stated in the press as declaring that the number of men under his command 'were not sufficient to keep back the Orangemen.'

Calls by a Protestant Justice of the Peace and by leading members of the town's Catholic community for extra police to be drafted into Portadown to deal with an Orange march in July 1873 went unheeded. The Orangemen paraded into the Catholic Obins Street area, provoking what one senior RIC man described as the worst riots he had witnessed anywhere in twenty years. Shots were fired by Orangemen and several business premises and many homes along the length of Obins Street were wrecked. Thirty three people were later charged with having taken part in an unlawful assembly and riot.

In December of that year, another Orange demonstration to commemorate the Relief of Derry and attended by upwards of 3,000 Orangemen was held in the town. Orangemen paraded into William Street where the Catholic Church and parochial house were attacked and other Catholic-owned property damaged. An attempt by the Orange parade to enter Obins Street was prevented by police.

Following appeals from Catholic businessmen and clergy in Lurgan, magistrates ordered the rerouting of an Orange parade away from the Catholic part of the town on July 12th, 1877. It was stated in the House of Commons that the parade had been rerouted in order to prevent any breach of the peace. No such rerouting was ordered in Portadown where RIC reinforcements were drafted in and concentrated in Obins Street to ensure free passage for an Orange parade through the area on the same date.

Serious rioting erupted in 1879 when Orange parades passed through Obins Street on Easter Monday. July also brought fresh outbreaks of trouble during an Orange march through the same area. There were more Orange riots in Obins Street in 1880 and 1882.

In 1883 questions were asked in the House of Commons regarding attacks upon the Catholic Church, Catholic homes and other Catholic-owned property in Portadown during an Orange march in that year.

Twenty seven people were charged with rioting and disorderly behaviour in Obins Street on the 12th and 13th of July 1886 when Orange marchers paraded through the district.

The conduct of Portadown Orangemen was again raised in the House of Commons in July 1887 when the Chief Secretary was questioned about an incident which occurred when the Orange Order had marched through Obins Street, under police escort, on their way to Drumcree on Sunday, July 10th. It was stated that a Catholic man had been seriously injured by Orangemen as the police looked on.

Nine men from the Obins Street area appeared in court on September 29th, 1891 charged with riotous behaviour. Most of the men were members of the nationalist 'Tunnel' Accordion Band. Apparently the Band had taken part in a nationalist protest against Orange marches being allowed into that area of the town. The chairman of the court said that he thought the Orange march should not have been in the area.

While a large contingent of armed RIC men ensured no trouble took place during Orange parades through Obins Street in July 1892, only 14 police were on duty in the area on the 13th July. An estimated 2,000 members of the Orange Order and Black Preceptory returning from the Sham Fight in Scarva were due to parade through the small Catholic enclave that evening. Immediately upon the parade's entry into the area, at 6.10pm, vicious rioting broke out, with the Orange and Black-men running amok in the area and Catholic residents attempting to defend their homes. In the face of desperate resistance the marchers retreated, only to attempt a second march at around 7.00pm. Again an intense period of rioting broke out which lasted around 30 minutes before the marchers were repulsed by the residents and the small RIC force. By 7.45pm the marchers again had regrouped ready for their third attempt to storm the area. This time they came armed and Catholics waiting for them at the 'Tunnel' bridge fled when fired upon. The Orange and Black marchers then made their way halfway along the street wrecking houses before the residents regrouped and charged them. The RIC, who had retreated to the barracks to arm themselves, reappeared and charged the marchers with fixed bayonets, driving the attackers out of the area for the third and final time. An extra 100 armed police were drafted into the area that night and more arrived the following morning.

On August 12th further trouble erupted in the town when the Apprentice Boys were prevented from marching through Obins Street. The Apprentice Boys were forced by police to take an alternative route. Marchers and their supporters then proceeded to attack Catholic-owned property around the town.

During the following years, however, large forces of police escorted the Orange and other marches through the Obins Street area, placing the local residents under a virtual state of martial law. Those in charge of policing obviously believed it was more prudent to capitulate in the face of Orange violence than to protect and defend the rights of the town's Catholic community.

The anti-Catholic nature of the Order again raised its head at the opening of Derryhale Orange Hall in July 1899. The ceremony was chaired by the Portadown District Master, W.J. Locke, who was also a Unionist politician and a Justice of the Peace. According to the local press, one speaker at the ceremony attacked those Portadown Protestants who employed, sold land or consorted with 'Papist rebels', and one businessman was accused of 'helping to plant Popery' in the town by selling land to Catholics 'on which to build a nunnery.'

In July 1900, Catholic homes in William Street and Mary Street, as well as St. Patrick's Hall in Thomas Street and the parochial house were attacked by Orange marchers.

A number of nationalists appeared in court as a result of disturbances which took place when an Orange parade passed through Obins Street in July 1903.

An Orange parade through Obins Street on Easter Monday 1905 resulted in a Catholic man being shot dead. Patrick Faloon, a 36 year old father of four was standing alone in Woodhouse Street when Thomas Cordner, a Protestant factory worker, produced a revolver and fired at him. Faloon ran for the cover of nearby John Street but was shot in the back and died in his Curran Street home shortly afterwards. Two RIC men grabbed Cordner as he was about to fire a third shot at Faloon. As Cordner was being led to the Barracks a crowd of Orangemen attempted to rescue him. A fierce riot then ensued between the RIC and several hundred Orangemen. That evening police blocked the entrance to Obins Street, forcing a second Orange parade away from the area.

Questions in the House of Commons concerning the activities of the Orange Order in Portadown were becoming almost as frequent as their parades through Obins Street. In 1909, Joe Devlin, the MP for West Belfast, asked the Chief Secretary if he was aware that every year the Orange Order marched, with police protection, through an exclusively Catholic part of Portadown – even though there was an alternative route open to them – and questioned him on whether or not he was aware that, on the 13th July, they had paraded yet again, with the indulgence of the police, in a provocative manner through Obins Street, cursing the Pope, and playing party tunes. He said that a number of people had been injured in scuffles and shots were fired by the Orangemen while passing through the area. Referring to the arch in William Street, Mr Devlin said that, to the annoyance of the Catholic residents of the street, Orangemen had been permitted to erect an arch only a few yards away from the Catholic Church, to parade playing party tunes, and to act in an most offensive manner opposite the Church.

Living Memory – Oppression and Violence

> Orange Order parades in the Obins Street – Garvaghy Road area have a history and tradition dating back to a time when nationalists raised no objections to the parades. (Orange Order statement, July 1995.)

In 1913, the annual general meeting of Portadown Unionist Club was told by the secretary, J.A.Wilson, that 12 divisions of the Ulster Volunteer Force had been armed with rifles. Wilson thanked the Orange Order for allowing their halls to be used for drilling and training purposes. The three strands of loyalism,

Orangeism and paramilitarism again led to another British government being forced to capitulate in the face of threats and undemocratic demands. This time the issue was that of Home Rule and through it, the possible loss of prestige and power that the Orange/Unionist leadership had enjoyed for so long.

With the partition of Ireland and the establishment of a Unionist government in the North, the role and power of the Orange Order had reached its zenith. Not only had the Order members in the actual government, its influence now spread through all walks of life, backed up by a fully armed militia in the form of the RUC and the notorious 'B' Specials, the members of which were almost exclusively Orangemen. A series of sectarian murders of Catholics carried out in County Armagh and elsewhere during the 1920's have been widely attributed to members of the 'B' Specials.

David Rock, a leading member of both the Orange and Black Institutions, was the District Commandant of the 'B' Specials in the years after partition. R.J. Hewitt, appointed Sub-Divisional Commander of the 'B' Specials in Portadown in 1943, was another leading Orangeman.

1931 saw major street disturbances in Portadown again. On Saturday 15th August a loyalist mob waited for the return of two buses bringing local nationalists back from an A.O.H. demonstration in Armagh City. The loyalists followed the buses to Obins Street where local people had assembled awaiting their return. Only a few police were on hand, and a riot ensued with the loyalists being forced away from Obins Street by the nationalists. The loyalist crowd then went on the rampage around the town, attacking and destroying Catholic-owned property and severely beating at least three nationalists. Such was the extent of the rioting that the local magistrates considered introducing a curfew. For the following week all pubs were closed at 7.00pm, people ordered off the streets at dusk, and no crowds were permitted to congregate. There were no more major incidents but, according to some people who can vividly recall that period, the local nationalist population felt as if they were in a state of siege for some considerable time afterwards.

In 1932 thousands of Catholics from throughout the Six
Counties travelled by train to Dublin for the International
Eucharistic Congress. Portadown was the central rail junction
for the North and, as the special trains approached Portadown
from Dublin on Sunday June 26 and the early hours of Monday
June 27, they were met with showers of stones, bricks, bottles
and other missiles. As well as the trains, Obins Street and
nationalist homes in other parts of the town also came under
attack.

Numerous incidents, mainly of a minor nature, took place
during the July parades in 1933 and 1934. Catholic children
returning from what was known locally as 'the Canon's trip' –
a day excursion organised by the local parish priest – were
forced to run a gauntlet of abuse on July 16th 1935 by hundreds
of Orange supporters. A number of women who had gathered
at the railway station to meet the children on their return from
the trip were assaulted. The following day, a full-scale riot was
sparked off when three RUC men were seen to assault a man at
the corner of Park Road and Obins Street. When several baton
charges failed to disperse the nationalist crowd, the RUC, under
the command of a County Inspector Dudgeon, then opened
fire. 56 year old Hugh Faloon, who was standing at the window
of his upstairs bedroom of his home in Obins Street, was fatally
wounded and died two days later. The volleys of shots dispersed
the crowd and many fled into their homes, where they were
followed by the RUC riot squads, beaten and then arrested.

Orangemen were stoned while passing through Obins Street
on July 12th, 1937. Some Orangemen were reported to have
been injured, but no other incidents are said to have taken place.

During the Second World War, no Orange marches took place
in the Six Counties and, for the first time since the establishment
of the Orange Order, Portadown experienced a decade relatively
free from civil and sectarian strife.

Eight nationalists were prosecuted as a result of what appeared
to be a peaceful protest during an Orange parade in Obins Street
on July 13, 1950. They were defended by Mr H. McParland,
who stressed that the defendants had merely attempted to walk
across the street where they lived while an Orange parade was

passing. He pointed out that there was an alternative route for the parade and if the alternative route was taken by the marchers, it would prevent trouble in the future. Under further cross examination, Head Constable Stansfield admitted that the local nationalist accordion band was confined to parading in Obins Street; defence counsel asked him did he not think that, in the interests of peace, the Orangemen should be confined to their own areas. Stansfield replied, 'It is not given to me to think... I am here to obey orders!' Four of the defendants were found guilty and fined. Despite Stansfield's admission in court regarding the assault, no Orangemen were prosecuted.

Head Constable Stansfield was a central figure in another court case in 1954 which arose out of an incident when a car was deliberately driven through a nationalist procession headed by St. Patrick's Band in Obins Street. A young woman was charged with 'indecent conduct'. Stansfield said that he went to break up a crowd of people who were hammering on the car when the young woman ran towards him. 'I put up my clenched fist with the gloves in it and she ran her face right into my knuckle', he stated. Defence counsel suggested that the police hadn't made adequate traffic arrangements, and pointed out that the nationalist band seemed to have a most unfortunate history of similar incidents. A lorry drove through it in 1948 seriously injuring a number of band members and supporters; on another occasion a bus drove through it; and in August 1952 a motorcycle crashed into it – quite remarkable given that the band was always confined by the RUC to parading along a 600 yard long stretch of one street! Nevertheless the law took its course and the young woman was convicted on an amended charge of disorderly behaviour – assaulting a policeman's fist with her face would not have looked right on a charge sheet.

During the 1950s and 1960s, local residents generally ignored the Orange marches through the nationalist areas of the town at the request of the local Catholic clergy. Some local people continued to attempt to protest at these annual provocative displays, but no major incidents occurred.

Development of Garvaghy Road and Civil Rights

The 1960s also saw the commencement of a major housing redevelopment programme in Portadown. Much of the older housing stock, particularly in Curran Street, John Street, Mary Street, River Lane, etc., was demolished and the new housing estates of Garvaghy Park, Churchill Park and Ballyoran Park were built along the Garvaghy Road. With the advent of 'the Troubles' the sectarian divide in housing became even more pronounced. This led to a situation along the Garvaghy Road which even the Orange Order admits:

> Where once Orangemen had walked along the Garvaghy Road to the gaze of no-one, they now walked past housing estates which were almost exclusively Roman Catholic and who resented the parade. (*The Orange Citadel.*)

Indeed, that same history also reveals that 'during the 1970s and early 1980s repeated attempts were made by the Roman Catholics of Obins Street and Garvaghy Road to prevent Orange parades from walking through these districts'.

July 14th, 1969 saw a crowd of 400–500 members of the Black Preceptory and their supporters lay siege to a public house in Woodhouse Street, where a young man from the Obins Street area was being held by the RUC. Fighting had broken out while the Black parade was going through Obins Street and the RUC had bundled the young man into the pub to save him from the mob. He was later charged with assaulting one of his attackers.

Many nationalists fled from Portadown in advance of the Drumcree and other Orange parades in July 1971. The Drumcree parade through Obins Street on Sunday July 4th saw a large number of the recently disbanded 'B' Specials lead over 1,000 Orangemen through the area. The nationalist areas were completely saturated by hundreds of RUC and British troops, in order to prevent any opposition to the marches.

UDA/UVF and Obins Street, 1972

All roads into Portadown were completely sealed off by loyalists and the Obins Street area was the subject of continuous assault by loyalist mobs from Sunday March 26th until Wednesday

29th March 1972 after the suspension of the Stormont government. In response, the extreme loyalist grouping, the Ulster Vanguard Movement, of which David Trimble was Deputy Leader, had called for a forty-eight hour strike. In the town centre, all known nationalist-owned businesses were wrecked and looted, and scores of Catholic families living in Protestant areas were intimidated and forced out of their homes. At the start of July, the UDA set up 'no-go' areas around the town. Within hours, a 47 year old nationalist disappeared. The tortured and mutilated body of Felix Hughes was found submerged in a drain leading to the River Bann four weeks later.

The Portadown Resistance Committee, which had organised the defence of the town's nationalist areas during the loyalist attacks, had made an appeal in April calling on the authorities to reroute the July parades. When further pleas for rerouting were ignored, local people began to erect barricades along Obins Street on Saturday 8th July in an attempt to prevent the first of those marches taking place the following day.

On Sunday 9th, a massive force of British troops, including Paratroopers, moved into the area to clear the route for the Orangemen. Scores of CS gas canisters and baton rounds were fired in order to quell opposition to the march. The RUC, who moved into the area behind the troops, smashed their way into homes along Obins Street, badly beating up the occupants. Having gained control of the area, the RUC and British army then permitted a large contingent of masked and uniformed members of the UDA and UVF to parade and drill in Obins Street. These hooded loyalists then lined both sides of the street and saluted as several hundred Orangemen marched through the district on their way to Drumcree. The same contingent of loyalists again accompanied the Orangemen on their return from Drumcree along the Garvaghy Road, where another massive British army deployment effectively suppressed any opposition from the nationalist residents.

The British army and RUC actions were carried out a time when a bi-partisan ceasefire was in operation between the IRA and the British, and were classed by the Republican leadership as a severe breach of the truce agreement which eventually totally disintegrated in the Lenadoon area of Belfast later that evening.

A similarly oppressive British army and RUC presence also ensured no opposition to the Orange marches through the area on July 12th and 13th. Within hours of the 12th parade taking place, a Catholic pub owner, Jack McCabe and one of his customers, William Cochrane, were shot dead by an off-duty RUC man in Portadown town centre. A Protestant youth, Paul Beattie, was also shot dead that morning on the Garvaghy Road.

Curfew 1975

The *Portadown News*, a local newspaper that was unionist in orientation, carried a description of what an Orange parade to Drumcree entailed for the town's nationalist population in July 1975.

> A visitor to the town could have been excused if he had been under the impression that a fair proportion of the British army stationed in Ulster had been drafted into the town, and an equally large proportion of strength of the Royal Ulster Constabulary.
>
> Right from the moment the procession of 1,000 men and three bands entered Woodhouse Street, there was an atmosphere of a town under siege. Soldiers armed with rifles, and officers equipped with high powered binoculars thronged the railway bridge. Scores of policemen flanked the entrance to the station itself...
>
> Inside Obins Street, it was a case of troops and police all the way to Corcrain with Saracens (armoured personnel carriers) and land-rovers in profusion and soldiers also prowling around with fierce-looking Alsatian dogs. As well as this, red-capped military policemen, green-clad Women's army, and of course Women's RUC were also to the fore, not to mention scores of plain clothes policemen and soldiers. All the time a helicopter whirred overhead, swooping down at times to survey the scene.
>
> Security measures from the top of Garvaghy Park to Parkmount were just as stringent as those on the outward parade. Saracens and soldiers crowded the grassy slopes of

the Ballyoran Park estate, and the entrance to Garvaghy Park. It was the same at Churchill Park where scores of police watched the perimeter and troops were on patrol in the alleyways.

All this for a 'church parade' which the Orange Order, even today, maintains has never caused controversy!

Given such extreme levels of saturation of the nationalist areas of Obins Street and the Garvaghy Road, any protests against the unwelcome Orange marches were effectively silenced. It should also be stressed that what amounted to the imposition of martial law and curfew within these areas lasted for up to a full week at a time, and not just for the length of time it took a parade to pass through.

For the next few years, the 'security presence' aimed at preventing any protests against the parades was maintained during July. This presence in turn led to minor outbreaks of rioting between local nationalist youths and RUC/British army, usually on the eve of a march.

Barricades were erected, plastic baton rounds and at least five shots were fired during serious clashes between nationalists and the RUC on July 13th 1981. The rioting, which lasted for several hours, broke out after the Orange Order had paraded through the area four times that day. A number of young men was subsequently arrested and charged by the RUC. At least 100 local residents took part in a peaceful protest against the marches the following day, July 14, when an estimated 1,500 members of the Royal Black Preceptory marched through Obins Street. A solid wall of RUC men lined the footpath along Parkside Flats where the protest was held.

At the trial of those arrested for the July 13th riots, a solicitor defending the young men said that what had happened in Obins Street was the inevitable consequence of allowing Orange parades to take place there. The Resident Magistrate, Mrs Sarah Creanor, said that she sympathised with the defence argument that Orange parades were an unnecessary provocation, and agreed that these parades should not be allowed into the area.

It was during the 1981 H-Block hunger strike protests that the first real attempt to develop an organised response to Orange parades through the area emerged. A small group began to research local history so as to refute Orange, RUC and local newspaper claims that disturbances around Orange parades were a recent phenomenon and inspired by republicans. Though they complained of having been harassed and receiving death threats from the RUC, who at the time were being accused of running a 'shoot-to-kill' policy, the group continued writing to newspapers and sent a petition with around 1,000 signatures to the Northern Ireland Office.

Despite the presence of the RUC and British troops in 1983, Orange marchers broke ranks in Obins Street and attacked local people at the bottom of Obins Drive. Several local residents had to receive medical attention after being assaulted by the marchers who used ceremonial swords and pikes to carry out the assaults. A serving member of the UDR was identified by locals as being the ringleader of the attack.

St. Patrick's Day Parade 1985

On the 17th March, 1985, the local nationalist St. Patrick's accordion band had intended to hold a parade from Obins Street to the Garvaghy Road. Despite their opposition to this parade in previous years, the RUC, to the surprise of many locals, gave the band permission for the St. Patrick's Day parade, including that portion of the route along Park Road. However, loyalists led by several Unionist councillors, including the then Mayor of Craigavon, Arnold Hatch, and Cllr Gladys McCullough, threatened to hold a counter-demonstration along the route of the parade. On Sunday morning, 17th March, a crowd of flag-waving loyalists gathered in the Park Road area with Unionist members of the Borough Council, supposedly to hold a 'prayer meeting'. As the band left Obins Street a large force of RUC personnel immediately moved in to block its path and senior RUC officers told the organisers that the parade could not proceed as previously agreed. Attempting to take an alternative route, the band was again blocked by the RUC. The band then left to go to a major St. Patrick's Day celebration in County Tyrone by bus.

That evening, on its return from Tyrone the band attempted to parade again along the route agreed with the RUC several weeks beforehand. There was no loyalist protest that evening. But the RUC attacked the band members and its followers, at one stage driving their armoured landrovers through the ranks of the band. The reaction of nationalists was one of outrage and anger. The RUC were shown to be using extreme force to defend the right of the Loyal Orders to parade along very contentious routes, at the same time preventing nationalists parading on what was a natural and only slightly contentious route. The result of St. Patrick's Day was to galvanise nationalist opposition to the July parades. Residents of Obins Street and the Garvaghy Road disrupted a meeting of Craigavon Borough Council in protest at the action of the Mayor and other Unionist councillors.

On July 5th, it was announced that the 12th and 13th parades through the nationalist district would be rerouted, but the Drumcree parade would be permitted to continue along Obins Street and the Garvaghy Road on July 7th. Local nationalist residents held a meeting on the 6th at which they re-iterated their demand for the rerouting of all the parades, and announced their intention to hold a peaceful demonstration in Obins Street.

On Sunday 7th, at around 9.30am residents attempted to hold a peaceful sit-down protest in Obins Street in a last minute effort to halt the parade. As the media looked on, 'the RUC waded into the protestors, batoning them without provocation', as one foreign journalist put it. Hand to hand fighting then commenced but, within 10 minutes, hundreds of RUC men in full riot gear had dispersed the protest and cleared the way for the 2,000 Orangemen, led by Unionist MPs, Harold McCusker and Rev. Martin Smyth. Among the marchers was the Belfast politician, George Seawright, who openly taunted and gestured at local people in a blatantly sectarian manner. On the return along Garvaghy Road, hundreds of RUC men in riot gear, backed up by troops, sealed off the entire length of roadway, refusing access to any but the Orangemen.

On the 12th and 13th, Orangemen and their supporters rioted in the town centre for several hours after those parades were rerouted.

Midnight March Easter 1986

On Easter Sunday, 1986 a ban was announced on an Apprentice Boys march due to take place the following day. From around 9.00pm on Sunday, hundreds of British troops and RUC men saturated the Garvaghy Road, apparently to enforce the ban. At 11.00pm, cars with loudspeakers toured the town calling on loyalists to assemble in the town centre in order to break the ban. Shortly before midnight, the British army and RUC presence was withdrawn from the Garvaghy Road without explanation and returned to barracks, despite the fact that thousands of loyalists were already gathered in the town centre. Over an hour later, approximately 4,000 loyalists led by Unionist politicians, including Ian Paisley, began to march along the Garvaghy Road.

Eye-witnesses stated that many of the marchers, who included known members of the RUC and UDR, openly carried fire-arms. Several RUC landrovers also accompanied the illegal march. As the marchers commenced to attack and wreck nationalist homes along the road, many local people attempted to defend their homes and families against the loyalist invasion. The RUC made no effort to prevent the attacks, turning instead upon the nationalists. Intense fighting broke out between local residents and the RUC, which lasted for several hours, and barricades were erected to prevent the RUC/loyalists from re-entering the area. It was widely believed at the time that the RUC in Portadown had mutinied and had refused to enforce the ban, or to prevent the illegal march taking place. No loyalists were ever prosecuted for participating in the illegal parade or the attacks upon nationalist homes.

Later, on Monday loyalists went on the rampage in the town centre, looting and wrecking shops and businesses, forcing the RUC to disperse them with plastic baton rounds. A loyalist youth from Lurgan, Keith White, was fatally wounded by a baton round and died later in hospital.

July 1986

In the run-up to the July parades in 1986, the Parade Action Committee and the Ulster Clubs, headed by leading Portadown Orangeman, Alan Wright, threatened major disruption if the Orange parades were prevented from going through Obins Street and Garvaghy Road. Alan Wright, along with the DUP's Peter Robinson, and Markethill man, Noel Little, (later to be arrested in Paris for offences linked with alleged loyalist/ South African gun-running activities) was soon to lead a parade of Ulster Resistance through Portadown.

The activities of the Parades Action Committee and the Ulster Clubs led to a concerted campaign of intimidation and terror throughout June. Nationalist homes and church-owned property came under constant attack. Shots were fired at local people from a car travelling along the Garvaghy Road. An Ulster Clubs' parade on June 16 resulted in several nationalist-owned shops being wrecked and St. Patrick's Hall, a Catholic social club in Thomas Street, was burned to the ground by the marchers. On the afternoon of Tuesday 16th, the town centre and many roads leading into the town were blocked by hi-jacked vehicles in a show of loyalist strength, and all shops were forced to close. Two further midnight marches, organised by the Ulster Clubs and the Parades Action Committee took place in the town on Thursday 19th and Tuesday 24th June. Throughout this whole period the RUC stood back as the local nationalist community was placed under a state of constant siege.

On Sunday 6th July, a massive concentration of RUC and British army were deployed in Obins Street and the Garvaghy Road to suppress nationalist protests against the Orange march to Drumcree. 3,000 troops and 1,000 extra RUC personnel had been drafted into the town. Prominent civil liberties activists from Ireland and abroad had been invited to Portadown by the local Sinn Fein councillor, Brian McCann. A protest by nationalists in Obins Street was the subject of an RUC banning order and prevented from even taking place. Over 300 people had tried to assemble at Parkside flats in Obins Street for the protest only to be faced with the total saturation of the district by the RUC. Another protest on the Garvaghy Road by the People Against Injustice Group was forcibly broken up to make way for the Orangemen. St. John's Catholic Church was attacked by Orangemen and their supporters while Mass was in progress and a Catholic priest assaulted at the bottom end of Obins St. Father Patrick Thornton received cuts and a swollen eye.

Once again, rerouting orders away from Obins Street were issued, this time for the 12th and 13th of July Orange and Black parades.

It was at this time that the British government and the RUC reached one of the most inexplicable decisions ever taken surrounding Orange marches in the town. Having decided that such marches would no longer be allowed to proceed through Obins Street, many nationalists believed the authorities would also take the next logical step – reroute the Orangemen away from the Garvaghy Road. However, logic would seem to have been in short supply. Far from rerouting the contentious Garvaghy Road march, the Orange Order were now told by the RUC that they could now have a second march along this route on July 12th.

This incensed nationalists. What the RUC were doing was making a deal with the Orange Order that if they accepted the rerouting of all marches away from Obins Street, the RUC would permit the Order to have a second, and completely new, march along the Garvaghy Road, where the bulk of the town's nationalist community lived.

On Friday 11th July, hundreds of loyalists attempted to force their way into Obins Avenue and Obins Drive after they were incited to do so following a speech by the extremist politician, George Seawright at an Eleventh Night bonfire in nearby Edgarstown. This violent onslaught on the area, during which at least two blast bombs were also thrown, lasted for over an hour before the RUC arrived on the scene. In predictable fashion, the RUC attacked local residents and provoked a riot with nationalists from the Garvaghy Road who were trying to make their way into Obins Street to assist the locals defending their homes from the loyalist mobs.

On the 12th morning, nationalists on the Garvaghy Road were once more assaulted and beaten by baton-wielding RUC men, as the Orangemen held their first ever Twelfth parade along the road.

1987 – No Drumcree parade on Garvaghy Road

During the next twelve months nationalists redoubled their rerouting campaign.

In July 1987 it was announced that the Drumcree parade would be completely rerouted from Obins Street. Nationalist protest was then focused solely on the Garvaghy Road and hundreds of local people gathered there from early on Sunday morning to take part in a sit-down protest against the Drumcree parade. The Orange parade did not materialise. Instead of marching to Drumcree, the Orangemen held a religious meeting at Corcrain Orange Hall as a protest at having to take the alternative route away from Obins Street. This clearly demonstrated to many people that the Orange Order could and would break with its hitherto sacrosanct 'traditional routes', and they argued that since the Order had voluntarily given up the Garvaghy Road once, they could do so again.

Nevertheless, the post-Drumcree 12th July morning parade went ahead as usual. As many people held the mistaken opinion that it too would not be taking place on account of the previous Sunday's non-event, the numbers who turned out to object were less than expected. A women's silent protest was prevented by the British Army from leaving Churchill Park to confront the marchers. The RUC were particularly furious with the women protestors, insulting them and ripping away their placards. One of the women was hospitalised.

1988 – 1994 Riots and Peaceful Protests

In June 1988 a planned parade by the Drumcree Faith and Justice Group from the Garvaghy Road into the town centre was restricted to a 400 yard stretch of the Garvaghy Road by the RUC. The organisers had told the RUC that only 30 people would take part and that the only symbol would be a banner with a green hand and an orange hand interlinked. The Drumcree

Faith and Justice Group had a Christian motivation and commitment to using exclusively peaceful means. They wrote to all the relevant authorities every year expressing their belief that the vast majority of residents were opposed to Orange parades on the Garvaghy Road and that the opposition was just and right on moral and religious grounds. The Orange Order in Portadown never acknowledged the receipt of a letter in the 8 years of their campaign.

In July the Drumcree Faith and Justice Group organised a sit-down protest on the road with only limited numbers taking part. The RUC removed the protesters forcefully to make way for a parade consisting of approximately 500 Orangemen and 4 bands, two church bands and two 'kick the pope' or 'loyalist' bands. Crowds of nationalist residents at Ballyoran, Garvaghy and Churchill were hemmed in by over 1,000 members of the British army and RUC. The road was lined with security vehicles. As one newspaper report recorded afterwards, 'only a massive show of strength from the police and the army ensured the Drumcree parade passed off without major incident'.

This was a pattern to be repeated for five years. Parades were preceded by nights of riots. Peaceful protests (cross-community tea party, loud music and limited sit-down protests) were suppressed by a very heavy security presence.

During the Drumcree parade in 1992, led by David Trimble MP and consisting of 1,200 Orangemen and four bands, marchers and bandsmen broke ranks on the Garvaghy Road and attacked several local people as well as a press photographer in full view of the RUC. The attack incensed nationalists hemmed in behind RUC lines and there was fighting between the RUC and locals at Ballyoran Park and also at Churchill Park/Woodside.

A survey carried out in the Garvaghy Road area by the Drumcree Faith and Justice Group in 1993 showed that 95 percent of those questioned were opposed to Orange marches along that road. But for the first time in years, there was no organised protest against the parades. There was, however, an increase in rioting in the area on the nights before the marches as young people, frustrated at the seeming ineffectiveness of previous protests, vented their anger on the police and property. In 1994 the Drumcree Faith and Justice Group failed to hold a protest. Opposition to the parade was only expressed by riots during two previous nights.

Drumcree Crisis – 1995

Public Meeting

By May 1995, local community activists were attempting to harness the resentment and anger which the Orange parades created into a constructive and peaceful campaign. This led to the formation of the Garvaghy Road Residents' Group, which was to act as an umbrella group of tenants' associations in the various housing estates, political parties and the Drumcree Faith and Justice Group.

The GRRG requested meetings with the Orange Order and with the RUC. Over 1,200 signatures were gathered for a petition that called for the marches to be rerouted. Despite several direct requests and the use of intermediaries, no response was ever forthcoming from the Portadown Orange District.

Meetings with local RUC chiefs throughout May, June and the first week of July were unsatisfactory. It became quite apparent that the RUC did not have a consistent policy on the issue of parades, or on the interpretation of the existing Public Order legislation and its application. Indeed, the RUC made it clear that the matter was one for the Secretary of State. A request by the GRRG to have a direct meeting with the RUC Chief Constable met with refusal.

The Residents' Group also wrote to the Secretary of State, Patrick Mayhew, asking him to use the powers available to him to prevent any Orange marches taking place along the Garvaghy Road. The response came from an official of the Security Policy and Operations Branch of the NIO who wrote: 'Decisions on the routing of parades are an operational matter for the RUC.' This reply totally ignored the powers available to the Secretary of State under the Public Order legislation, and conveniently disregarded the precedents set by Douglas Hurd in banning Orange parades from Obins Street a decade earlier.

Having failed to receive any assurances that the marches would be rerouted, the GRRG filed the statutory seven days notice with the RUC of their intention to organise a protest march from the Garvaghy Road to Carleton Street Orange Hall on the morning of Sunday 9th July.

The RUC then asked for two meetings with the Group on Tuesday 4th and Friday 7th at which the RUC requested that the residents reconsider both the timing and manner of their protest. It was pointed out to the RUC that public meetings of residents had fully endorsed the protest and that the RUC had offered no legitimate reason why the protest could not go ahead as planned.

Local RUC officers removed two dozen Irish tricolours from the Garvaghy Road area on the Thursday night before the Drumcree Parade. During the same week, the Mid-Ulster Brigade of the UVF issued a statement, published in two local newspapers, saying they would be 'closely monitoring the controversial parades in the area.'

On Sunday morning, July 9, it became clear that the community's desire for peaceful opposition to the Orange marches was being heeded. For the first time in over twenty years, there had been no rioting in the nationalist areas on the night before a march.

At around 9.50am, the residents' protest march made its way from the junction of the Garvaghy and Ashgrove Roads towards the town centre. It was halted shortly after 10.00am, several hundred yards further along the Garvaghy Road by the RUC. The protestors then made their way back to the junction of the Garvaghy and Ashgrove Roads where they remained at both sides of the road. As time went by the numbers of those taking part in the residents' protest increased. From mid-day onwards RUC vehicles approached the protestors, and senior RUC officers, including Assistant Chief Constable Hall, asked the organisers what their intentions were and if they intended to block the road. The RUC were told that that depended on whether the Orange march would be allowed down the

Garvaghy Road, or whether the RUC would attempt to restrict the movement of local people to their homes and streets. Just before 12.30, the protest organisers were asked by the RUC to inform residents that landrovers would be advancing towards them but would stop about 50 yards away. The organisers then called everyone together to inform them of what was about to happen, and not to panic. They informed them that they should all move back towards the footpaths again. Immediately afterwards, Chief Superintendent McCreesh told the organisers that the residents had broken the law by blocking the road and were liable to prosecution, even though McCreesh knew that the organisers were relaying Assistant Chief Constable Hall's message. This was clearly a deliberate attempt by the RUC to artificially manufacture a public order situation. The response of the residents was unanimous – if they were going to be accused falsely of blocking the road, there was only one legitimate response; several hundred people moved out from the footpaths and promptly sat down on the roadway. RUC landrovers then took up position on either side of the sit-down protest and the residents anxiously awaited the next move, knowing as they did that the return parade from Drumcree would be due to commence shortly after 1.00pm.

At Drumcree the RUC told the Orangemen their march along the Garvaghy Road would not be able to proceed as planned due to the nationalist sit-down protest. The Portadown District Master then announced that the Orange Order would remain at Drumcree until such time as they could march the Garvaghy Road.

At 4.45pm, ACC Hall relayed a message to the Residents' Group via Superintendent Blakely that the Orange march had been rerouted and would not be going back into town along the Garvaghy Road. Members of the GRRG then addressed the nationalist protestors who, by then, numbered around 700. Urging them to support the next protest on July 12, they asked the residents to disperse peacefully and not to go near any possible flashpoint areas.

Less than a mile away, Harold Gracey, the Portadown District Master, had issued a call for Orangemen across the North to show their solidarity by blocking their own towns and villages. As Gracey made this announcement, the notorious Portadown loyalist, Billy Wright, was already organising a blockade in Charles Street close to many nationalist homes. The local Unionist MP, David Trimble, also read out a statement which called for 'all Orange brethren to muster at the church'. Throughout the afternoon and evening, sporadic violence erupted at Drumcree as Orangemen and their supporters attempted to break through towards the nearby nationalist Ballyoran Park estate. The arrival of Ian Paisley brought the announcement of a massed rally of Orangemen to be held on Monday night.

In the meantime, Orangemen and their supporters seized control of all roads around Portadown and effectively put the town's nationalist community under siege, and prevented access to or exit from the nationalist area. Nationalist families living along Charles Street and the Dungannon Road were particularly isolated and vulnerable during the following days and nights, as thousands of Orangemen commenced illegal parades past their homes to and from Drumcree while the RUC looked on. The vulnerability of these nationalist families was graphically demonstrated when a nationalist family of four was burned out of their home in Corcrain that night.

On Monday it was clear that the Orange and Unionist leadership were not seeking a resolution of the issue. Instead they were gearing up for confrontation, concentrating their energy in organising the massed rally planned for 7.30pm that night. Elsewhere Orangemen and their supporters, in response to Harold Gracey's call, were beginning to block roads across the North. Larne Harbour was closed by Orangemen led by their local MP, Roy Beggs. Protests took place in Belfast, Carrickfergus and other parts of the North.

The Secretary of State astounded many people that afternoon when he tried, Pontius Pilate-like, to wash his hands of the increasingly serious situation. The former Attorney General gave a curious interpretation of his legal responsibilities: 'It's not for me, I have no role in this at all. I'm certainly not going to act as an adjudicator or arbitrator or anything of that sort; that's quite unconstitutional.'

An offer from the Garvaghy Road Residents' Group seeking a meeting with the Orange Order in Portadown Town Hall that evening to discuss the Twelfth parade was rejected. Independent mediators were then asked to put the GRRG's proposals to the Order.

The massed rally which started at 8.30pm and was attended by approximately 10,000 people, led to a major deterioration of the situation in Portadown. A series of speakers, including several Unionist MPs, addressed the rally. However violence erupted almost immediately following a speech by Ian Paisley when he urged his assembled audience to 'win this battle or all is lost; it's a matter of life or death, freedom or slavery.'

Over 1,000 loyalists, many wearing Orange sashes and other regalia, broke through the RUC lines which offered only minimal resistance. The loyalists veered towards Ashley Close and Andre Heights, launching a barrage of missiles at the houses and their terrified occupants before directing their attention towards the nearby St. John the Baptist Primary School. In Craigwell Avenue, beside which a loyalist blockade had been in place from Sunday, almost all the nationalist families had no choice but to leave their homes after the RUC repositioned their landrovers and allowed loyalists access to the street. When confronted by residents of the street about this, the RUC officer in charge stated 'my men are not prepared to protect the likes of you'. (When questioned later about the incident by a GRRG delegation the Chief Constable said they could not identify the officer involved.)

By 10.30pm the general mood within the nationalist community was reminiscent of 1969, with families genuinely afraid for their safety and preoccupied with the question of their defence. At 12.30am the mediators returned from their meeting with the Orangemen. It emerged that Ian Paisley and his son, along with David Trimble, were negotiating on behalf of the local Orangemen. It was also becoming clear from other sources that in order to end the riot at Drumcree, the RUC was arranging a deal with Paisley and Trimble to allow a march to take place along the Garvaghy Road at 2.30am. The GRRG immediately prepared to organise another sit-down protest on the roadway to thwart the RUC/Unionist deal.

At around the same time reports were coming through to the GRRG meeting that a large crowd of loyalists, estimated to be between 800-1000, led by the figure known as 'King Rat', had made their way from the town centre to Obins Street/Park Road and the public park. Dozens more nationalist homes were now placed under threat and open to attack at any time. RUC units which had been positioned in Woodhouse Street, supposedly to pre-empt such a move, drove their vehicles into a carpark and let the loyalists pass unhindered.

Within an hour around 500 people had returned to the scene of Sunday's protest on the Garvaghy Road. Shortly before 3.00am, a force RUC riot squad arrived to confront the nationalist protestors. Under the glare of television spotlights, the RUC officer in charge was challenged to state why he intended to forcibly move peaceful nationalists while those Orangemen who had caused mayhem around the town were still allowed the freedom to assemble at Drumcree and other points in Portadown. By 3.30am the RUC riot squad had pulled back.

Shortly after 5.00am, in the presence of mediators, negotiations recommenced directly between the GRRG and RUC Divisional Commander Heuston and Superintendent Blair. The mediators then went to the Orange Order. The two RUC Deputy Chief Constables, Ronnie Flanagan and Blair Wallace, took over negotiation for the RUC at 9.00am. The outline of a negotiated settlement was emerging. During this part of the proceedings Flanagan responded positively to the mediators' proposal that there would be no more parades on the Garvaghy Road without the consent of locals.

It was agreed that only local members of Portadown Orange District would parade without bands or banners. The protestors would move to the footpath on the approach of the Orangemen and allow them to pass. It was understood by all that no Orange march would take place on the Garvaghy Road on the Twelfth.

The agreed Orange march took place at 10.50 on Tuesday morning. However, as it passed by the nationalist protestors, it was quite evident that the marchers included many Orangemen from other towns. Within minutes of the marchers leaving the Garvaghy Road, the Orange and Unionist leadership denied any agreement had been made. David Trimble, who along with Ian Paisley joined the marchers as they left the Garvaghy Road, was the first to deny the existence of the agreement:

> There was no compromise. We have come down our traditional route in normal fashion with our flags flying.

In Carleton Street, Orangemen formed a guard of honour for Trimble and Paisley who then victoriously pranced, hands joined and held aloft, to the entrance of the Orange Hall.

On the 12th morning, District Master Harold Gracey announced that the Portadown lodges had decided not to march along the Garvaghy Road in order 'not to cause any further hassle to their fellow citizens' – a frank if somewhat understated recognition of the reality of the situation. Nevertheless, nationalists remained somewhat sceptical of this apparent overnight change of heart.

That scepticism proved well-founded when an Orange lodge, led by a band, approached the Garvaghy Road from the town centre and paraded around Woodside Green, a mixed but predominantly nationalist housing estate. Protestors then blocked the Garvaghy Road to prevent the Orangemen going any further. The nationalists succeeded in turning the parade back towards the town, but serious questions were asked as to why the RUC had let the parade into the area in the first place.

The behaviour of the Orange and Unionist leadership, coupled with the fact that the nationalist community had endured almost 48 hours of siege, terror and intimidation, enraged many local people. It was obvious to all that it would be extremely difficult for the Orange Order to win the consent of the residents of the Garvaghy Road area for some time to come.

Silence is Orange

In an effort to prevent a repeat of the summer's events, the Garvaghy Road Residents once more wrote to the Orange Order seeking a meeting around the beginning of September. Again no reply or acknowledgement was forthcoming.

The Mediation Network was asked by the residents to attempt to facilitate a meeting with the Orange Order in Portadown. Despite spending several months trying to arrange such a meeting, and spending long hours preparing the GRRG to meet the Orange, the Network came up against a brick wall of refusal.

The Orange Order continued to revel in triumphalism after July. Medals were struck to commemorate the 'Seige of Drumcree' and at a special ceremony in September, David Trimble, Ian Paisley, Harold Gracey, Jeffrey Donaldson and the Church of Ireland rector at Drumcree, Rev John Pickering, were awarded the first of these medals for their part in the 'Seige'. Referring to the mis-spelt medals, local people suggested that those who so vociferously demanded to walk the Queen's highway should at least have a grasp of the Queen's English.

September also saw David Trimble elected as leader of the Ulster Unionist Party. After his victory, Trimble was carried shoulder high from the building by two Portadown Orangemen.

That autumn, the committee changed its name to the Garvaghy Road Residents' Coalition. This was done to acknowledge the fact that it included representatives of several groups based within the town's nationalist community. The Coalition then began to contact as many interested parties and individuals as possible to put forward their case for the rerouting of Orange parades away from the Garvaghy Road. Meetings were held with leading members of the Alliance Party, Mo Mowlam of the British Labour Party and with Sinn Féin, amongst others.

David Trimble, leader of the Unionist Party and Member of Parliament for the constituency in which the Garvaghy Road lies, was also contacted. Three letters were sent to Trimble from November onwards, but he completely ignored them.

The Secretary of State was also asked around the same time to meet the residents. Sir Patrick Mayhew's willingness to address meetings of the Orange Order in Comber, County Down, and other places, was in stark contrast to the response sent by his office to the Residents' Coalition: a meeting 'would serve no useful purpose at this time'.

1996 crisis

In January, a delegation of the Residents' Coalition met with leading members of the Presbyterian Church at Church House in Belfast. This exchange of views with the Presbyterians, who included four former Moderators of the Church, was felt to have been very constructive.

In the same month a similar delegation of residents met the RUC Chief Constable, Sir Hugh Annesley, Deputy Chief Constable Blair Wallace, Assistant Chief Constable Fred Hall along with 'J' Divisional Commander, Terence Heuston. The RUC chiefs were questioned on their apparent inability to police the situation in Portadown the previous July, and the failure to prevent thousands of Orangemen coming into the area from outside Portadown. The Chief Constable accepted that the overwhelming majority of people living in the Garvaghy Road area were opposed to the Orange parades. He also accepted that the GRRC represented the views of the residents.

However, Annesley went on to suggest that there was no guarantee that the events which had taken place in Portadown with regard to the Orange parade and subsequent demonstrations in '95 would not happen again. When the residents asked if the RUC was prepared to stand by the assurance which DCC Flanagan had given the mediators the previous July (that no parades would take place without the consent of the residents), they were met with silence. The Chief Constable said that the primary responsibility was with the two disputing parties and he felt the onus was on us to resolve the issue. He accepted that we had made every effort to meet with the Portadown Orange representatives.

The Church of Ireland Primate, Archbishop Robin Eames, agreed to meet a delegation of residents' representatives. The meeting in Armagh appeared to be the most positive one to date, with the Archbishop telling the delegation that he was hopeful of being able to arrange a meeting between the residents and the Orange Order. Nevertheless, at Easter, Eames was to inform the residents that his attempts to facilitate a meeting had ended in failure.

At the end of May, Coalition representatives met with Deputy Chief Constable Flanagan and Assistant Chief Constable Hall. Flanagan denied having made any statement the previous year to the mediators concerning future parades along the Garvaghy Road. However, he said that, unlike in other years, a decision would be announced as to whether or not the Drumcree parade could go ahead several days beforehand.

June saw the beginning of prosecutions against nationalists for their part in the anti-parade protests of the previous July. Five people were due to appear in court on charges of 'hindering the free flow of traffic'. Only one case went ahead while the rest were adjourned for another several months.

The two day hearing against the chairperson of the Residents' Coalition, Breandán Mac Cionnaith, was eventually thrown out by the magistrate. The magistrate criticised the Crown Prosecution for having brought the case in the first place, saying, 'I have not seen anything at all that would remotely approximate to support this charge'. He went on to describe evidence given by several RUC witnesses as being 'flimsy and nebulous'.

The GRRC, meanwhile, had engaged legal counsel in order to institute High Court action to prevent the 1996 Drumcree march from proceeding, and a number of legal challenges were planned by the lawyers.

On June 27, less than a fortnight before the planned Orange march was due to take place, the GRRC called another public meeting in Ashgrove Community Centre. Over 800 people attended the meeting, many of whom were unable to get into the actual centre. Those present unanimously voted in favour of holding peaceful protests in the event of the authorities deciding to allow the contentious parade to go ahead.

On Wednesday July 3, the GRRC held a meeting with DCC Flanagan and ACC Hall in Belfast. For most of the meeting,

Flanagan tried to paint a bleak scenario of what would happen should the Orange march be rerouted. He made it known that the Orange Order had an organised plan ready to put into operation if the march did not get going down the Garvaghy Road. The residents asked what the RUC decision was to be but he refused to answer, saying it would be announced within the next 48 hours.

On Thursday July 4, around 500 people took part in the first of a series of protests on the Garvaghy Road against the Orange march due on the 7th. The protest, which took the form of a roadside picket, stretched for half a mile along the road.

On Friday morning, the world media gathered at RUC Headquarters to hear the decision concerning Sunday's Orange march. They were disappointed. The RUC said that the announcement was delayed until the following day, as 'negotiations' were ongoing. This came as a surprise to the Residents' Coalition as they had not had any contact with the RUC, or anyone else, since Wednesday.

On Friday afternoon, the residents commenced their legal bid in the High Court to force the Secretary of State to use the powers available to him to ban the march. The judge hearing the case adjourned until Saturday, pending the outcome of the RUC announcement.

That evening a second protest was held on the Garvaghy Road. The crowd was larger than the night before, with somewhere in the region of 800 people taking part.

On Saturday morning, the residents returned to the High Court in Belfast to resume the adjourned legal action. At the same time, the RUC Chief Constable, Hugh Annesley, held his delayed press conference. When announcing the rerouting of the Drumcree march away from Garvaghy, Annesley told the press that there was a perfectly acceptable and viable alternative route available to the Orange Order – an argument nationalists in Portadown had been making for years. Given this decision, the residents' legal action was not pursued, and they issued a statement saying that all activities planned by the GRRC were now cancelled.

The Grand Master of the Orange Order, Martin Smyth MP, condemned the RUC decision and in a strange twist to the history of the situation in Portadown said: 'It is actually bowing to an element who have orchestrated the last two years this protest, whereas in previous years, it had gone without any problem' (*Sunday Life* July 7). The Mid-Ulster UVF issued a grimly worded statement which hinted at its intention to use force: 'There is a feeling on the ground that we have reached the point of no return'(*Sunday Life* July 7).

On Saturday July 6, 1996, over 2,000 British troops and RUC men were deployed in Portadown. On Sunday morning, larger than usual numbers of Orangemen took part in the Orange march to Drumcree, with the local MP, David Trimble, at its head. Following the church service, the Orangemen paraded towards the RUC lines and then returned to outside the church where their leaders addressed them. Harold Gracey told the Orangemen that, in a few hours, they would see protests happening throughout the North. Orange Grand Master, the Rev Martin Smith told the assembled throng: 'Drumcree is not isolated. If you think you can isolate it you have made a grave mistake. There can be no compromise.' Ian Paisley was in his usual blood curdling form when he arrived in the afternoon: 'We are fighting for the promise of the life to come, and that's worth fighting for and that's worth dying for.'

Across the Six Counties, roads were blocked. Orangemen and their supporters seized control of all roads around Portadown and the town's nationalist community was effectively isolated. As night fell, Orangemen and their supporters made several violent and unsuccessful attempts to break through the barbed wire entanglements at Drumcree.

Murder

A nationalist taxi-driver was murdered during the hours of darkness by loyalists, widely believed to be members of the Mid-Ulster UVF. The body of 31 year old Michael McGoldrick from Lurgan, the father of a seven year old girl and whose wife was expecting their second child, was not discovered until

Monday morning. The following day a message faxed to the GRRC office, in a chilling and ominous reference to the McGoldrick murder stated quite simply:

1 DEAD, 5,999 MORE TO GO.

On Monday July 8 only a few hundred Orangemen remained at Drumcree. Almost all shops and businesses in Portadown were forced to close on Monday following threats from loyalist paramilitaries. All roads into town remained closed and many vehicles were hijacked and burned. Main roads across the North, including the M1, M2 and the main Belfast-Dublin road were blocked. Larne Harbour and Belfast International Airport were blockaded.

No attempts were made by the RUC or British army to prevent Orangemen marching out to Drumcree from the town centre. Nationalists living in Craigwell Avenue, Charles Street and along the Dungannon Road were the targets of constant abuse by these marchers. Several thousand Orangemen and supporters again gathered at Drumcree that evening, and once more there were sporadic outbreaks of violence. As darkness fell, Orangemen used a powerful public address system continually during the night to prevent residents in the nationalist areas from sleeping in a not-so-subtle attempt at psychological warfare. The, by now, familiar sectarian chant of 'we're going to burn Garvaghy, we're going to burn Garvaghy' was heard clearly across the fields.

BAYING FOR BLOOD

While the Orange Order leaders would prefer to distance themselves from the talk of ethnic cleansing and the outbreaks of lawlessness which they have blamed on 'sinister elements', some of those dark forces are within their own ranks. Standing in the holy grounds around the beautiful Drumcree church, one Orangeman, who admitted to being a loyalist paramilitary, said he would not only die for the right to march down the barricaded road, but would go much further... [He] told me: 'We have to burn the Catholics out and kill their children with swords. All of them.'

In case I hadn't heard him... he repeated it. 'You think I'm joking. Well I'm not. It may sound extreme but if you don't kill the kids they will grow up and will be killing you. We must have them all out'.

Report by Kim Willsher, *Sunday Mail* (USA) 12th July 1998.

On Tuesday morning, July 9, the GRRC received a telephone call from Peter Smyth of the Northern Ireland Office. The NIO were seeking a private, off-the record meeting. Wary that the NIO might later deny the meeting, the GRRC asked Smyth to put the request in writing. The NIO then faxed a letter through which was signed by J.M. Steele. Steele's letter said the purpose of the discussions 'would be to get a first-hand impression of the feelings of the local community at this particularly tense period; and to explore what, if any, room for manoeuvre the association sees as existing now or in the future.'

The Residents' Coalition sent a reply to the NIO setting out points for discussion, including the rerouting and the feelings of the local community. The Coalition's response also pointed out that any Orange march down the Garvaghy Road that year was 'currently viewed as totally unacceptable and not open to discussion.'

Right across the North, Orangemen and their supporters continued with their blockades. Reports were being received by the media that many of these blockades were taking place with the apparent collusion of the RUC in many places.

On Tuesday, Breandán Mac Cionnaith received a request from the Church of Ireland Primate, Archbishop Robin Eames, for a meeting. This took place at 9.15am on Wednesday July 10 and lasted for around 30 minutes. Mac Cionnaith said that the Residents' Coalition had been trying for over a year to enter into dialogue with the Orange Order on the parades issue without any response. Archbishop Eames then said he might still be able to arrange a meeting with the Orange Order, but nothing definite was agreed.

At 11.10am on Wednesday, a residents' delegation consisting of Breandán Mac Cionnaith, Eamon Stack, Joe Duffy and Laura Boyle met Northern Ireland Office officials in the local community centre. Present for the NIO were John Steele, Peter Smyth and Ms McGimpsey. The consensus of the Residents' Coalition was that the NIO had offered nothing of substance to the local community. A response to that effect was then sent to the NIO. Indeed, it was the feeling of the GRRC delegates that the NIO, and by implication, the British government, clearly were in favour of an Orange march going ahead. It is most likely that the decision to force the Orangemen down the Garvaghy Road was made at government level in the immediate aftermath of this meeting.

Mutiny

Meanwhile at Drumcree, Orangemen had produced a mechanical digger which was driven in and out of Drumcree on three separate occasions. At no time did the RUC or British army attempt to stop or seize the machine on its journeys. At its second appearance, steel sheeting had been placed around the cab. The British army then responded by bringing up their own 20-ton bulldozer which was supported by a 10-ton truck. Still no attempt was made to seize the digger. Orangemen at Drumcree cheered loudly in response to an announcement over the P.A. system that two companies of the Royal Irish Regiment, based at Mahon Road Barracks in Portadown, had refused to leave the barracks for duty that afternoon.

Shortly after 5.00pm, Archbishop Eames phoned Breandán Mac Cionnaith asking him to nominate three people to meet the Orange Order. Cardinal Daly met the Residents' Coalition at 8.00pm in Churchill Park, Portadown. During the course of this meeting, a fax arrived from Dr Eames outlining several proposals. When Cardinal Daly read the fax, he informed the residents that these proposals were not what the other three church leaders had agreed to earlier in the day. He indicated that the Orange Order was offering nothing that would leave the nationalist residents with their dignity intact. The Cardinal voiced his support for the alternative route put forward by the GRRC.

The Residents' Coalition stated that they would be willing to participate in a meeting with the Orange Order, provided only members of Portadown District attended and that it be co-chaired by Cardinal Daly and Archbishop Eames. They also proposed two main items for an agenda: discussion and agreement on the issue of parity of esteem and the principle of consent to be accepted by the Orange Order in relation to all future marches; only in the event of agreement on these issues, would the Residents Coalition be willing to discuss what Archbishop Eames had described as 'the current dilemma'. The Coalition also made clear that any proposed agreement would have to be endorsed and accepted by the community.

There was then a lot of to-ing and fro-ing as Archbishop Eames tried to set a time for the meeting. It was eventually agreed that the meeting would take place in the offices of the Ulster Carpet Mills at 9.00am the following day.

However, it would soon become apparent that another train of events was in motion elsewhere that effectively was to make this meeting redundant. Shortly after the appearance of the RUC's Deputy Chief Constable, Ronnie Flanagan, at Drumcree that night, Harold Gracey and Ian Paisley addressed the crowds of Orangemen assembled there. Both men were extremely confident that the Orange Order would be marching along the Garvaghy Road. Around the same time, many of the RUC and British army vehicles which, up until then, had been facing the Orangemen, were being redeployed during the hours of darkness to face towards the nationalist enclave.

David Trimble, held a secret meeting with leading Mid-Ulster loyalist, Billy Wright, in an upstairs room of Drumcree Church Hall. It is widely believed that Trimble afterwards conveyed an assessment of the paramilitary threat from the Mid-Ulster UVF to the British Secretary of State, Patrick Mayhew.

Early on Thursday morning, July 11, members of the GRRC arrived at their temporary headquarters in Churchill Park to prepare for the 9.00am meeting at the Carpet Mills. From 7.00am onwards they were continually bombarded with questions from media personnel regarding the front page report in that morning's edition of the *Belfast News Letter*. The paper's headlines carried a stark warning: DRUMCREE DEAL AFTER LATE-NIGHT TALKS: MARCHERS READY TO HIT ROAD TODAY. The Residents' Coalition issued a statement saying that no deal had been done which involved them.

The three residents' delegates, Breandán Mac Cionnaith, Joanna Tennyson and Eamon Stack entered the building at

9.00am and were met by Archbishop Eames and Cardinal Daly. Over the next two hours as the residents waited to meet the Orange Order representatives, it became clear that the whole idea of a meeting had been a complicated ploy to lull nationalists into a false sense of security, and an attempt to ensure that their community's leadership was kept out of the way.

Shortly after 11.00am, the GRRC delegates received telephoned reports of major RUC movements at Drumcree Road. They then asked to speak to the Church leaders. The residents then entered the room where the churchmen were waiting, and informed them that they were leaving and returning to Churchill Park. They stated that, in their opinion, the meeting had been a complete sham. On leaving the building, the residents' delegates were told that the Orange representatives had already left earlier. At no stage were the residents ever informed of this fact.

By the time the three reached Churchill Park, the RUC was already preparing to force a passage for the Orangemen through the area. Several hundred local residents congregated on the Garvaghy Road, with a large force of RUC personnel in full riot gear less than fifty yards away from them. One member of the Residents' Coalition, Joe Duffy, who had asked to talk to a senior RUC officer, was hit by a police baton and suffered a concussion and a head wound. He was later hospitalised. His was to be the first of many injuries received at the hands of the RUC that day.

Many local people were enraged at the RUC and government's complete and utter capitulation to the Orangemen's demands and threats of force. They sat down on the roadway and chanted their defiance at the Order, the government and its forces: 'No Sectarian Marches, No Sectarian Marches'.

Chief Superintendent McCreesh approached the residents' spokesperson in order to talk to him. Mr. McCreesh's first words were 'I had no part in this – I'm only carrying out orders'. He was told the Nazi SS had once used the same excuse and the conversation was closed. A few minutes later Mr. McCreesh approached the sit-down protestors. His attempts to speak were drowned by locals chanting 'SS RUC'. In response, he turned around and waved his blackthorn stick at the men under his command. It was the order for the RUC to commence one of the worst displays of sectarian thuggery witnessed since 1969. Age or sex did not matter as hundreds of RUC men, heavily clad with body armour, mercilessly attacked the protestors from three sides. Men, women and children were assaulted and dragged screaming from the roadway and thrown behind a row of armoured landrovers. They were the lucky ones.

Wooden RUC batons crashed into the limbs and skulls of others. Even hardened journalists were repulsed at what they bore witness to, as the crack of breaking arms and legs could be heard clearly above the cries of the innocent. In a few minutes, the road was clear and sealed off by a double line of landrovers. In those few minutes at least fifty people had suffered broken limbs, head wounds and other injuries which required medical treatment.

But the RUC's orgy of violence had not ended. When the Orange march victoriously turned from Drumcree Road onto the Garvaghy Road, two lines of RUC men with shields and batons charged the residents again. Beating them into the estate, the RUC commenced firing volley after volley of plastic bullets at everyone within range while a small group of youths threw stones in response. There followed indiscriminate volleys of plastic baton rounds, causing even more injuries.

As the march made its way towards the town centre where thousands of loyalists had gathered, shock and disbelief on the Garvaghy Road turned to fury as nationalist youths tried to respond to the RUC's actions by throwing anything on which they could lay their hands. The series of events was vividly described by one mother of three children from Churchill Park: 'This community, the Garvaghy Road community, was raped'.

The British Prime Minister (Major), the Secretary of State (Mayhew) and the Chief Constable (Annesley) all united in saying that the decision to force the parade through was purely a 'professional' public order issue decided without interference by the Chief Constable. Annesley claimed his decision was based on preventing killings: 'I would not have traded one life for the Garvaghy Road.' But one man's life had already been traded – that of 31 year old Michael McGoldrick, murdered by loyalist paramilitaries acting in support of the Orange Order at Drumcree. Hours before Annesley's interview was broadcast, another life was traded for the Garvaghy Road, that of 35 year old Dermot McShane in Derry, crushed beneath a British army Saxon carrier. More were to be killed.

The events of July 7-11, 1996 could have been avoided. In the previous year the Garvaghy Road Residents' Coalition made many attempts to enter into a genuine dialogue with the Orange Order. All those attempts were spurned and rejected. Even the local MP and Unionist Party Leader, David Trimble, opted to 'ride the wild horses of hatred and sectarianism' (*Irish Times* Editorial July 13, 1995) rather than enter into dialogue to resolve this issue. The British Secretary of State also saw 'no useful purpose' in discussing the matter with local residents.

1997

(Abridged and updated version of *Looking into the Abyss: Witnesses' Report from Garvaghy Road, Portadown, July 4-6, 1997*, Boston, PeaceWatch Ireland, November 1997)

Following the 1996 Drumcree stand-off, the British government appointed a Commission to look into the legislation governing parades and marches, and the respective responsibilities of the Secretary of State, the Chief Constable of the RUC and others. The North Report, published in January 1997, recommended the setting up of a Parades Commission which would seek to resolve marching disputes locally and would have powers to issue rulings, including whether or not marches should go ahead and under what conditions. Authority would revert to the RUC when it came to 'public order' considerations.

The Parades Commission was appointed by Secretary of State Mayhew in March 1997. The Chair was Alistair Graham, the former General Secretary of the British trade union, the Civil and Public Services Association. The Commission's remit, however, was restricted to education, promoting mediation and the development of a code of conduct. Just a month later, Robert Hamill was attacked and stamped on by a 30-strong group of loyalists in full view of four RUC officers sitting in a landrover just 20 yards away. The attack occurred late at night in the centre of Portadown as Hamill and three others (including two of his female cousins) were walking home from St. Patrick's Hall. He died eleven days later.

The 'radical and far-reaching' step (as Mayhew called it) of the Parades Commission taking over the RUC's decision-making powers with respect to parades and marches had to wait until the fall of the Conservative government and the arrival of the New Labour administration and Secretary of State, Mo Mowlam. The Commission did not acquire the new powers until after July 1997 and 'Drumcree III'. Mo Mowlam made a personal visit to Garvaghy Road residents in May and gave public assurances that she would let them know her decision on whether the parade could proceed. At a subsequent meeting with residents and their legal representative at Stormont a few days before the Drumcree parade, Rosemary Nelson reminded the Secretary of State of that promise and said they needed fair warning of the decision in case the residents wished to lodge a judicial review. Mowlam again said she would personally let the residents know what the decision was. This did not happen. PeaceWatch Ireland take up the story.

When the PeaceWatch Ireland delegation arrived in Portadown on Friday, July 4 (1997), Garvaghy Road residents still did not know whether the upcoming Orange march would be re-routed around their neighbourhood or if it would be forced through. Although the security forces had begun to set up checkpoints around Portadown, they had not yet established a presence in the vulnerable Obins Street/Craigwell Avenue area, where 16 Catholic families had their homes invaded and wrecked by loyalists led by Billy Wright in the previous year's violence. At 6pm, over 800 residents held signs (such as 'No Talking/No Walking') in a picket line that stretched almost the full length of the road – from Ballyoran Heights, where the tents of the Women's Justice Encampment had been pitched, to Churchill Park, where a series of murals were being painted in full view of the road. After the picket, residents gathered to hear an update from local independent councillor Breandán Mac Cionnaith, who said that he had no new information and cautioned residents not to engage in excessive drinking or provocative behaviour.

In the early evening, three PeaceWatch witnesses present on Craigwell Avenue saw security forces pulling up tanks and armoured landrovers. The RUC officer-in-charge said the security forces were 'just here to protect the Catholic community'. Meanwhile, witnesses also observed uniformed members of the RUC chatting in a friendly manner with civilians sitting on a wall 50 yards away from Craigwell Avenue. Local residents identified these civilians as loyalists and told PeaceWatch witnesses they felt that the loyalists' presence on Craigwell Avenue during the run-up to the march was inappropriate and intimidating, and that the RUC's comfortable relationship with the loyalists was cause for their extreme distress.

On Saturday morning, three witnesses met with Portadown RUC Superintendent Morris Bailey. According to Bailey, 'We (the RUC) are caught in the middle – no one more than us wants this settled.' He also said he had instructed his officers to treat international observers 'as well as they treat citizens – with respect.' Over the course of Saturday afternoon and evening, our witnesses saw increasing signs of a military and RUC presence.

At 6pm, the picket again took up its position along Garvaghy Road for about an hour, although the picket was held for a shorter length of time so that residents could attend evening mass. Councillor Mac Cionnaith told assembled residents that although Mowlam had said in news reports that she was engaged in an 'ongoing discussion' with Garvaghy Road residents, he had heard nothing from her since the previous Wednesday (July 1), nor any indication from the British government about whether the Orange march was to be re-routed or forced through.

He again warned residents to avoid alcohol and to restrain themselves from provoking loyalists or security forces. About 40 international observers then gathered at a Saturday evening dinner at the community centre to review the protocol by which the delegates from the Republic of Ireland, South Africa, Canada, and the US as well as members of the European Parliament agreed to abide. Two PeaceWatch witnesses attended evening mass, counting over 50 military vehicles in the church parking lot.

At about midnight, our witnesses saw about a dozen armoured military landrovers and at least three flatbed trucks loaded with bales of razor wire drive up Charles Street towards the Drumcree church. Following the convoy, British army troops in camouflage put down razor wire by the Drumcree church. This sighting prompted rumours in the community that the Orange march was going to be blocked. On that assumption, many media and observers went back to hotels in Belfast and did not witness the critical events in the early morning hours.

Our witnesses later noted an escalating sense of tension and anxiety in the community, fuelled by the absence of any news or clear signals from Mo Mowlam about whether or not the march would occur. The women's encampment was tense, with no singing, as women worried about their children's whereabouts; some left briefly to check on their teenaged sons. Mac Cionnaith, local independent councillor Joe Duffy, and other community leaders walked Garvaghy Road and the parkland areas trying to limit alcohol intake and urging any visibly inebriated residents to go home. Constant helicopter activity overhead and military vehicles on local streets fuelled wildly conflicting rumours: that the march itself was coming through under cover of darkness or that it had been called off altogether. Residents had set up a battery-powered air siren to alert the community if any military actions were sighted. The alarm was sounded at 1.30am when residents saw troops march down Garvaghy Road. Residents flooded into the street to sit on the road before the security forces would have a chance to block it. The troops turned abruptly onto Drumcree Road. When no further troops appeared, exhausted residents went back to bed. Some were visibly upset by what they felt to be an orchestrated manoeuvre by the security forces and suspected that it had been a deliberate false alarm.

Just before 3.30am, in full darkness, two PeaceWatch witnesses observing events on Craigwell Avenue heard a convoy of trucks and other vehicles moving rapidly up Charles Street towards St. John's Church. At the intersection of the Garvaghy and Drumcree roads, witnesses saw security forces outfitted with body armour, riot shields and batons invade Ballyoran Heights. Without any warning or opportunity for residents to retreat, British troops already had knocked down the Women's Justice Encampment, trampling the tents in an assault later justified as a search for petrol bombs and other weapons.

Witnesses also saw rows of armoured landrovers moving onto Garvaghy Road at high speed, taking up position six abreast with a narrow chute in the middle, in an attempt to close off access to the road from either side. In response to the siren, sounded for the second time, residents were flooding onto the road to sit down ahead of the armoured landrovers. The security forces fired plastic bullets not only on the road but at the bystanders who were watching but not sitting on the road as part of the nonviolent protest. In addition, witnesses saw troops firing plastic bullets into the housing estates.

Two witnesses who cut through the adjacent Ballyoran parkland to the Drumcree Community Centre saw that the security forces – including troops with machine guns – had spread throughout all the housing estates simultaneously and had blocked off Ashgrove Road. At the community centre, people who had been injured either by plastic bullets or batons were getting bandaged. People gathered there and saw the first inaccurate television news reports that the RUC and British army were responding to the violence of a nationalist riot, rather than initiating the blockade and attacking unarmed sit-down protesters.

Two other PeaceWatch witnesses, who at 3.30am were stationed further down Garvaghy Road at the intersection of

Ashgrove Road, later described the sudden onset of noise and panic as people began screaming in terror, the pervasive smell of diesel fumes and the surrounding roar of military vehicles. Residents streamed into the road to sit down before it could be closed by security forces. At the crest of the hill, witnesses saw landrovers taking up their positions on Garvaghy Road at high speeds while masked black-clad security forces in full riot gear operated in tandem: a line in front pushed residents roughly off the road with their plastic shields and beat them with batons, while immediately behind them marched troops armed with plastic bullet guns. They started firing plastic bullets, shooting indiscriminately down the road.

People were running from the armed troops and, when hit, staggered off the road. Hundreds of plastic bullets were fired, and we saw the security forces aim at close range and directly at head or chest rather than below the waist, in violation of their own official policy on the use of plastic bullets.

A few residents were seen throwing wood, rocks, soda cans, bricks, empty bottles and whatever else came to hand – including clods of dirt – at the security forces. There was a smattering of petrol bombs. At one point, residents lit several lines of gasoline in the road between themselves and the security forces; the RUC's fireproof coveralls allowed them to walk through the flames unimpeded.

At the intersection of Garvaghy and Ashgrove roads, over 100 residents – including two local elected officials – sat in a circle surrounded by troops. For over an hour there was a tense standoff, as the sit-down protesters said the rosary aloud and members of a Welsh nationalist choir sand 'We Shall Overcome' and other songs of solidarity. For a while, the security forces left an opening in the circle opposite the corner of Ashgrove and Garvaghy, and people were able to move on and off the road. There was palpable hostility in the atmosphere. One RUC officer swung his baton at a clearly identified PeaceWatch witness, forcing him to fall off the fence from where he was observing. Another RUC officer aimed a homophobic epithet in the direction of other PeaceWatch Ireland witnesses.

Then the security forces suddenly – and again without warning – moved to surround the circle and close it off, corralling residents while troops moved in to clear them. Protesters were beaten and dragged off the Garvaghy Road, kicked and thrown onto Ashgrove Road; family members who tried to come to their aid also were beaten. A teenage girl's pants were pulled off as she was carried out, and another woman's shirt was ripped open, exposing her breasts. Residents later reported to us that the RUC used the epithets 'Fenian bitch' and 'Fenian scum' as they threw people to the ground. Councillor Duffy was beaten so badly he required hospitalization, Councillor Mac Cionnaith was struck when he tried to locate his daughter in the circle. Local RUC superintendent Morris Bailey was observed inside the circle giving orders and our witnesses also noted that about half of the RUC present had no badge numbers visible.

Residents and observers were pushed into Churchill Park and tanks moved right up against the walls and doors of homes. Meanwhile, the RUC and military leadership refused to respond to solicitor Rosemary Nelson and other advocates and observers who tried to enter the area while protesters were surrounded at the intersection and while they were being beaten. One PeaceWatch Ireland witness called an ambulance to come to attend to the injured and was told by the dispatcher that the RUC were not allowing ambulances into the area.

The residents of Garvaghy Road were blockaded into their homes or their immediate neighbourhoods until the Orange march had passed in the mid-afternoon, a period of several hours. Many were blocked from rejoining family and friends trapped in adjacent housing estates, as the estates were separated and sealed off from one another by hundreds of RUC and machine gun-carrying British soldiers.

At about 8am, Garvaghy Road residents began trying to find a route to St. John's Parish Church, which stands at the head of Garvaghy Road. For three-quarters of an hour, residents took different paths toward the church and found themselves blocked by the security forces at every turn. About 200 frustrated parishioners finally gathered in one place, surrounded by armoured personnel carriers and armoured landrovers, while a local priest, Father Eamon Stack, attempted to negotiate with the security forces, but they refused to give parishioners access to St. John's. Father Stack and several local priests – including the pastor of St. John's Parish Church – then presided over a mass held in front of the Churchill Park housing estate, against a wall of military vehicles. 'It's just like in the Penal days,' said one resident defiantly. At the moment in the mass when the congregation traditionally makes a sign of peace by shaking hands with their neighbours, a priest and a resident made the extraordinary gesture of shaking hands with members of the security forces.

As the hour for the march approached, two PeaceWatch witnesses walked up to Dungannon Road to await the arrival of the Orange Order. At about 11am, about 2000 marchers appeared. The march moved to Drumcree church, entered the Drumcree church and later marched down Drumcree Road to Garvaghy Road. Morris Bailey was at their head as RUC escort. Soldiers with sighted rifles stood guard, their guns pointed towards Garvaghy Road.

When the Orange Order finally reached the Garvaghy Road at about 1pm, a noisy protest greeted the marchers, as residents banged trash-can lids, pots and store grates in the traditional nationalist gesture of defiance. Residents also unfurled a banner reading 'Mo-Mayhew: No Change' – a reference to Mo Mowlam and to former Secretary of State for Northern Ireland Patrick Mayhew, who had declined to intervene on behalf of the residents in previous marching conflicts on Garvaghy Road.

When the security forces started to withdraw at about 3pm, after twelve hours of occupation, residents chased them up the road, throwing rocks and hurling epithets. Some residents pulled up chunks of concrete from the street to heave at the retreating vehicles. In response, troops fired hundreds more plastic bullets.

On Sunday night, Garvaghy Road and other towns across the North reacted with unrest to the security forces' assault on Garvaghy Road. Nationalist anger escalated after newspapers published the 'game plan document', an internal government memorandum to Secretary of State for Northern Ireland Mo Mowlam. The memo, leaked to the press the day after the march, indicated that the British government had decided three weeks earlier to push the march through – to develop a strategy 'for getting some Orange feet on the Garvaghy Road' as 'the least worst outcome.'

Cat-and-mouse confrontations between nationalists and security forces continued over the next two days in Portadown and elsewhere. On Monday night, helicopters with no lights hovered over Garvaghy Road firing flares. The security forces re-occupied part of Garvaghy Road; British soldiers crouched in the bushes with machine guns, tanks occupied the Churchill Park end of Garvaghy Road. Nationalists fought back with construction debris and burned hijacked vehicles. PeaceWatch witnesses heard sounds of live ammunition but could not ascertain the source.

On Monday morning at 3am, Colleen McNally, a Garvaghy Road resident, was beaten by the RUC while walking home through People's Park. She was surrounded by approximately 70 RUC and thrown to the ground on her stomach; she later reported to PeaceWatch witnesses that she feared she would be raped. She then was arrested on spurious charges of assaulting the RUC and held for several hours before being released.

On Wednesday following the Orange march and the ensuing riots, the Garvaghy Road Residents' Coalition held a peaceful rally attended by about 10,000 nationalists from all over the North. As supporters boarded a bus to return home, the bus was attacked by loyalists and a woman was injured.

The following Sunday, the community gathered for Feile na mBoithre (street festival) that the Coalition had planned to stage during the afternoon of the Orange march. It was a community festival for families, with music, games, face-painting and few speeches. 'We are a people who've looked into the abyss', Mac Cionnaith said, 'but we decided not to cry, but to sing.'

1998

The start of the year was marked by widespread loyalist violence and murder. Just before the new year, on December 27th, INLA prisoners had killed Portadown LVF leader Billy Wright, imprisoned for intimidating a witness. This was used by loyalists as an excuse for a spate of eight murders from January onwards. Among these was the LVF sectarian murder of Adrian Lamph in the centre of Portadown, a killing carried out two weeks *after* the 'Good Friday Agreement'.

In June, the Parades Commission made its first adjudication on the Drumcree parade. It announced on the 29th that the return leg of the 5th July parade was re-routed away from the Garvaghy Road. From this date onwards and up to the time of this book going to press (early June 1999), the Orange Order has mounted a continuous protest at Drumcree and has held more than 180 rallies and parades on the fringes of the nationalist area of Portadown, many of them illegal and in contravention of Parades Commission rulings. During a loyalist riot in Portadown on September 5th, RUC Constable Francis O'Reilly was hit by a blast bomb, an action claimed by a group calling itself the Red Hand Defenders. He died a month later from his injuries. The same group claimed to have killed Brian Service (a Catholic from North Belfast) on 30th October.

Since the Orange Order declared its defiance of the Parades Commission Drumcree 1998 ruling there have been numerous attacks on Catholics and their homes in Portadown and elsewhere. The worst of these was the petrol bombing of a house in Ballymoney in which three young boys, the Quinn brothers, burnt to death on July 12th. Several others have been hospitalised and some of those living on the edge of the Garvaghy area have been forced to abandon their homes. The British Prime Minister's Office and Tony Blair himself have become directly involved in separate discussions with the residents and the Orange Order, which still refuses to meet the residents.

1999

Human rights lawyer Rosemary Nelson was murdered by a car bomb on 15th March. There were immediate suspicions that the conspiracy to kill her goes beyond the group which claims responsibility, the Red Hand Defenders. The device was thought to be too sophisticated for this group to be acting alone and local people raised questions about the behaviour of the military and RUC in the days and hours before the killing. This included helicopter surveillance over Rosemary Nelson's home. Police later confirmed that 'collusion' (between RUC/British Army and loyalists) is an aspect of the inquiry. It is clear that the tireless and respected lawyer had become a thorn in the flesh of the RUC. Two days after her murder, loyalist Frankie Curry, allegedly an intelligence source for the RUC, was shot dead in Belfast. Rumours then circulated that Curry was involved in the Nelson murder.

Rosemary Nelson acted for a number of families and individuals involved in 'high profile' cases. She had represented Garvaghy residents since 1995 and was part of a residents' delegation to Downing Street in January 1999 which presented Blair with a dossier on illegal parades and intimidation. She was also acting for the Hamill family and in May of 1997 had announced legal action against the RUC officers who observed, and failed to prevent, the Robert Hamill attack. In October 1997 she gave evidence to the UN's Special Rapporteur on the Independence of Lawyers and the Judiciary, Param Curamaswamy. Rosemary Nelson told the UN that she had received several death threats from the RUC via her clients and had lodged a complaint with the Independent Commission on Police Complaints. The ICPC initiated an investigation, conducted by the RUC, towards the end of 1997. By July 1998, the ICPC was sufficiently disatisfied with the RUC's inquiry that representations were made to the Secretary of State. The result was that Commander Mulvilhill of the London Metropolitan Police was appointed to oversee the inquiry into the death threats. All of this was revealed to Rosemary Nelson's family within a few weeks of her murder.

Not only was the UN aware of the threat to Rosemary Nelson's life: the personal safety of the GRRC and their legal representative had been specifically raised with 10 Downing Street. Blair's Chief of Staff, Jonathan Powell, met residents for proximity talks on the 18th July 1998 and was told of the delegates' concerns, especially since loyalists issued a leaflet threatening both Mac Cionnaith and Nelson. The NIO later offered security measures to two of the residents' committee because they were elected representatives, but Rosemary Nelson did not qualify in the eyes of the NIO. Ironically, the security measures for Duffy and Mac Cionnaith were being installed the very weekend of Nelson's murder.

When the UN Special Rapporteur raised the issue of threats against lawyers, including the mounting evidence of collusion in the killing of lawyer Pat Finucane ten years ago, at a meeting with RUC Chief Constable Flanagan, he was told that such allegations were part of an orchestrated campaign of malevolent propaganda against the RUC by republicans. Furthermore he could not guarantee the safety of those lawyers who had given evidence to the UN and were named in the draft report. The advice was to remove the names, which included that of Rosemary Nelson. In a report published in March 1998, Cumaraswamy called on the British government to take threats against lawyers seriously and to hold an independent inquiry into the murder of Pat Finucane. This was rejected by Tony Blair in a letter to the Law Society for England and Wales because 'there are no grounds to hold such an inquiry'.

Throughout 1999 calls for an independent inquiry into the Finucane killing grew. They are now joined by the demand for an inquiry, free from RUC control, into all aspects of Rosemary Nelson's murder.

In May, David Trimble finally met with the GRRC for the first time. On 4th June a fresh round of proximity talks began in Belfast between the Orangemen and the GRRC. That night, loyalists attacked two houses in the mainly Protestant Corcrain estate with blast bombs, killing 59 year old Elizabeth O'Neill. She had lived on the estate for 36 years and was married to a Catholic.

Conclusion

If the Orange Order ever did have any 'right' to parade with its symbols and emblems down the Garvaghy Road, by its triumphalist behaviour after 1995, its 'victory' parade to Carlton Street Orange Hall, and its refusal to meet the representatives of the local community on this issue, it forfeited that right.

Two alternative routes do exist for the Orange Order to march to and from Drumcree. The first is from the town centre via Corcrain Road, Charles Street, and Dungannon Road, returning by that route. The second is from the town centre via Loughgall Road, Corcullentragh and across to the Drumcree Road, again returning by this same route.

The first is the route put forward by the GRRC since 1995 as an acceptable compromise. Even though the march passes nationalist homes and a Catholic Church as it goes along Charles Street and the Dungannon Road, this is regarded by this community as the least contentious of the routes through the nationalist area of Portadown. When this compromise was proposed it was sincerely believed that this route offered a comparable level of dignity to both the Orange Order members and the nationalist community. However, given what occurred in 1996 and subsequently, particularly in the aftermath of many loyalist attacks on homes along this route, it may be difficult to convince many nationalists that even this compromise affords residents any real dignity.